Sung Cho

# DEFENDING AGABUS AS A NEW TESTAMENT PROPHET

A CONTENT-BASED STUDY OF HIS PREDICTIONS IN ACTS

# DEFENDING AGABUS AS A NEW TESTAMENT PROPHET

## A Content-Based Study of His Predictions In Acts

Sung Cho

Copyright © 2018 by Christian Publishing House

support@christianpublishers.org

All rights reserved. Except for brief quotations in articles, other publications, book reviews, and blogs, no part of this book may be reproduced in any manner without prior written permission from the publishers.

Write support@christianpublishers.org

ISBN-13: **978-1-945757-85-3**

ISBN-10: **1-945757-85-X**

 Christian Publishing House

Cambridge, Ohio

*DEFENDING AGABUS AS A NEW TESTAMENT PROPHET: A Content-Based Study of His Predictions In Acts* by Sung Cho

# Table of Contents

CHAPTER I ............................................................. 1
INTRODUCTION ................................................... 1
   Purpose and Occasion for the Study ................... 2
   Presuppositions of the Study ............................... 5
   Scope of the Study ............................................... 6
   Approach of the Study ......................................... 6
CHAPTER II ............................................................ 8
VIEWS CONCERNING AGABUS' PROPHECIES ...... 8
   Fallible NT Prophecy View ................................... 8
   Infallible NT Prophecy View .............................. 22
CHAPTER III ........................................................ 35
FAMINE PROPHECY OF AGABUS ....................... 35
   Nature of the Famine Prophecy ........................ 37
   Fulfillment of the Prophecy ............................... 55
CHAPTER IV ........................................................ 68
IMPRISONMENT PROPHECY OF AGABUS ......... 68
   Nature of the Imprisonment Prophecy ............. 70
   Fulfillment of the Prophecy ............................... 81
CHAPTER V ......................................................... 98
CONCLUSION ..................................................... 98
   Summary of the Preceding Discussion ............... 98
   Implications for the Modern Church ................ 100
BIBLIOGRAPHY ................................................. 105

OTHER BOOKS BY CHRISTIAN PUBLISHING HOUSE ........................................................................ 117

# CHAPTER I

# INTRODUCTION

Did the prophet Agabus make mistakes in his prophecies? The traditional view is that Agabus' prophecies were fulfilled in its details. However, some scholars have argued that the inferior nature of the NT prophetic gift provides possibilities for mistakes. The debate continues today.

In the book of Acts, Agabus plays a minor but important role. At first, he appears in Antioch with other prophets and prophesies about a famine (Acts 11:27-30). Later in Acts, Agabus reappears in Caesarea (Acts 21:10). After tying himself up, he predicts that the Jews will bind and hand Paul over to the Gentiles (Acts 21:11). Though both times he predicts a major event, very little is known concerning Agabus.

Even if he is not a major figure in Acts, Agabus is an important figure in the study of NT prophecy. His importance is due to the relative scarcity of prophetic content from NT prophets.[1] The largest body of prophecy in the NT is the Apocalypse, which was written by an apostle, not a prophet. Descriptions of NT prophecy in the epistles are limited to explanations of its nature, function, or role (1 Cor. 14:3, 6, 22; Eph. 2:20). As a result, Agabus' prophecies are unique phenomena of the non-apostolic prophetic gift.

In studying the prophecies, an important assessment concerns the accuracy of their fulfillment. Were the

---

[1] Acts 13:1-2 is another place where prophecy might have been uttered, but the identity of the spokesman is unknown.

prophecies of Agabus fulfilled? If they were fulfilled, to what degree of accuracy were they fulfilled? Agabus' prophecies in Acts 11:27-30 and Acts 21:10-11 can be examined for evaluation.

## Purpose and Occasion for the Study

The purpose of the study is to evaluate the accuracy of NT prophecies given by Agabus by measuring their precision of fulfillment. There are several reasons for this study at this occasion. First of all, the ongoing debate between cessationists and non-cessationists necessitates a study of the prophetic gift. The beginning of the controversy can be dated 1901, when the Pentecostal doctrines and denominations began to be formulated, with the charismatic movement and the "Third Wave" arising at the second half of the twentieth century.[2] All three camps emerged to encourage the practice of speaking in tongues, prophecy, and healing. However, cessationists from Reformed and dispensationalist backgrounds countered, denying the existence of such gifts today.[3] With these various divisions, there are at least two, perhaps as many as five positions concerning the practice of spiritual gifts near the end of the twentieth century.[4] So then the broad question of whether spiritual

---

[2]For a review of the three movements in the twentieth century and the major figures, see Wayne A. Grudem, "Preface," *Are Miraculous Gifts for Today? Four Views* (Counterpoints; Ed. Wayne A. Grudem; Grand Rapids, MI: Zondervan, 1996) .11-12; Thomas R. Edgar, *Satisfied by the Promise of the Spirit* (Grand Rapids: Kregel, 1996) 12-14; F. David Farnell, "Is the Gift of Prophecy for Today? Part 1: The Current Debate about New Testament Prophecy," *BSac* 149 (1992) 299-303.

[3]Grudem, "Preface," 10-11.

[4]Thomas Edgar observes that all of the three 20th century movements adhere to the belief that the practice of most, if not all spiritual gifts, should be encouraged today, as seen in Acts. The controversy of the "Spirit-baptism" post-conversion experience subsided once the cessationist/non-cessationist issue burgeoned. Edgar, *Satisfied*

gifts are active and practiced today provides the backdrop for this study.[5] A more focused question would be whether the gift of prophecy practiced today is in accord with the Scriptures. Such questions necessitate a study of NT prophecy.

Another important factor is the special interest in the study of prophecy that arose in the modern and postmodern era.[6] Key scholars hold that the condemnation of the Montanists (late 2nd century adherents of Montanus and his prophetic revelations) marked the end of major prophetic movements until the 20th century.[7] However, major developments in scholarship garnered interest in the study of prophecy near the end of the 19th century, beginning with the discovery of the *Didache* in 1873 and culminating with Grudem's *The Gift of Prophecy in the New Testament and Today* in 1988.[8] With the belief of "direct spiritual revelations" prevailing in churches worldwide and creating schisms among denominations in

---

*by the Promise of the Spirit*, 14. Grudem however, separates the "Third Wave" view from the Pentecostal and charismatic movements and also considers a great number of believers who consider an "open but cautious view." Grudem, "Preface," 13.

[5]A gamut of scholarly works and opinions are represented from both the cessationist camps and the non-cessationist camps. For a sample, see Dennis M. Swanson, "Bibliography of Works on Cessationism," *Master's Seminary Journal* 14 (2003) 311-27.

[6]For a list of works that illustrates the recent surge of interest, see footnote 4 in Farnell, "Is the Gift of Prophecy for Today? Part 1: The Current Debate about New Testament Prophecy," 279.

[7]Farnell, "Is the Gift of Prophecy for Today? Part 1," 295; D. A. Carson, *Showing the Spirit: A Theological Exposition of 1 Corinthians 12-14* (Grand Rapids: Baker, 1987) 166; David Hill, *New Testament Prophecy* (New Foundations Theological Library; Atlanta: John Knox Press, 1979) 190. For various opinions on why the Montanists were condemned, see David F. Wright, "Why Were the Montanists Condemned?" *Themelios 2* (September 1976) 15-22; David E. Aune, *Prophecy in Early Christianity and the Ancient Mediterranean World* (Grand Rapids: Eerdmans, 1983) 338.

[8]Farnell, "Is the Gift of Prophecy for Today? Part 1," 297-99. See also, Aune, *Prophecy*, 1-14.

the 21st century, the issue appears far from being settled.[9] How scholars define prophecy has implications for many Christians.

Finally, the last important factor that occasioned this study is the current neglect of content-focused study of prophecy. Understandably, the neglect is rooted in the difficulty of denotation when it comes to presenting a definition of prophecy. For example, Michael Green and D. A. Carson both lament that there are many answers to the question: What is prophecy?[10]

Due to the lack of uniform opinion in evaluating prophetic content, David Hill dismisses the content-study approach because he believes it is not possible to determine what exactly prophecy is.[11] He prefers to study the function of the prophet rather than work through studies of etymology, word studies, or content.[12] Furthermore, recent works on prophecy have been concentrated on didactic passages such as 1 Cor 12-14 where function, rather than the contents of prophecy are emphasized.[13] Yet, a content-based study of prophecy

---

[9] Philip Jenkins, *The Next Christendom: The Coming of Global Christianity* (New York, NY: Oxford, 2007) 73.

[10] Green presents the various ways to define NT prophecy: 1) a prediction; 2) something resembling the Apocalypse; 3) a formal appointment to an office (1 Tim 4:14); 4) a tool for evangelism, edification, consolation, or teaching (1 Cor 14). Michael Green, *I Believe in the Holy Spirit* (Grand Rapids: Eerdmans, 1975) 169-70; D. A. Carson, *Showing the Spirit* (Grand Rapids: Baker, 1987) 91.

[11] David Hill, *New Testament Prophecy* (New Foundations Theological Library; Atlanta: John Knox Press, 1979) 3-4.

[12] Ibid.

[13] Wayne A. Grudem's *The Gift of Prophecy in 1 Corinthians* (Washington: University, 1982) became the impetus for *The Gift of Prophecy in the New Testament and Today* (Westchester, IL: Crossway Books, 1988). See also aforementioned Showing *the Spirit* by Carson, and Robert L. Thomas, *Understanding Spiritual Gifts: The Christian's Special Gifts in the Light of 1 Corinthians 12-14* (Chicago: Moody Press, 1978).

may contribute to the study of NT prophecy and this approach will be attempted in this study of Agabus.

## Presuppositions of the Study

Several assumptions will be made for this study. First of all, the inerrancy and the inspiration of the Word are assumed, whether the views represented are sourced in the cessationists, the non-cessationists, or "the broad middle ground" of undecided believers. Debates concerning prophecy and spiritual gifts in general have been within the confines of this conviction.[14]

Consequently, the historicity of Acts is not questioned.[15] It is maintained that the book of Acts is a historically accurate account written by Luke similar to other biblical narratives.[16] Since Lukan narratives are

---

[14]Wayne A. Grudem, "Preface," *Are Miraculous Gifts for Today? Four Views* (Counterpoints; Ed. Wayne A. Grudem; Grand Rapids, MI: Zondervan, 1996) 19.

[15]If the testimony of Acts is not reliable, it would be difficult to ascertain whether its contents can be trusted as actual events. The historicity of Acts was not questioned until early 19th century, when Wilhelm Martin Leberecht de Wette, F.C. Baur and the Tubingen School emerged. Baur had an especially important role in influencing Zeller, who denigrated the trustworthiness of Acts in its details. For an overview of important proponents and critics of Acts' historicity in general and Baur's *tendenzkritik* in relation to Acts, see W. W. Gasque, *A History of the Interpretation of the Acts of the Apostles* (Peabody, MA: Hendrickson, 1989).

[16]Discussions concerning the genre of Acts have been many and closely linked with the historicity of Acts. For example, some have asserted that the book of Acts is a novel (Pervo) or a more complex hybrid-type of genre such as a "narrative of beginnings" with an apologetic aim (Marguerat). R. I. Pervo, *Profit with Delight: The Literary Genre of the Acts of the Apostles* (Philadelphia:Fortress, 1987); D. Marguerat, *The First Christian Historian: Writing the "Acts of the Apostles"* (Translated by K. McKinney, G. J. Laughery, and R. Bauckham; Society for New Testament Studies Monograph Series 121; Cambridge: Cambridge University Press, 2002) 33-34. For a defense of the view that Acts is a historical monograph, see Ben Witherington III, *The Acts of the Apostles: A Socio-Rhetorical Commentary* (Grand

critical in the study of prophetic content, these assumptions cannot be compromised.

## Scope of the Study

This study will be intensively focused on the foretelling accuracy of Agabus' prophecies. Other bodies of prophetic material such as Revelation will not receive full attention. In addition, all of the questions concerning the characteristics and functions of NT prophecy will not be explored save one: do the prophecies of Agabus have foretelling accuracy? This query is possible because prophecy is clear intelligible speech and Luke records the content of Agabus' prophecies, either directly or indirectly.[17]

## Approach of the Study

The approach to this study will be exegetical in nature. The Lukan account of Agabus' prophecies will be compared with the events of fulfillment. In the next chapter, the two major views concerning the accuracy of Agabus' prophecies will be defined and explored. One camp allows for fallibility in the NT prophets, while the other explicitly denies any possibility of mistakes. Therefore, it is necessary to outline the biblical rationale of the representative scholars in both camps.

Then in the third chapter, the first prophecy of Agabus will be examined where he predicts a famine in Acts 11:28. Luke's summary of Agabus' prophecy will be analyzed, concentrating on phrases such as ἐσήμανεν διὰ

---

Rapids: Eerdmans / Carlisle, UK: Paternoster, 1998) 2-39; Brian S. Rosner, "Acts and Biblical History," *The Book of Acts in Its Ancient Literary Setting* (ed. Bruce W. Winter and Andrew D. Clarke; The Book of Acts in Its First Century Setting 1; Grand Rapids: Eerdmans, 1993) 65-82.

[17]Green, *I Believe in the Holy Spirit*, 170.

τοῦ πνεύματος (signified through the Spirit) and ἐφ' ὅλην τὴν οἰκουμένην (upon the whole world). Then, a study of the subsequent narratives of Acts is pertinent to this prophecy. Also important are the various Greco-Roman sources relating the famines during Emperor Claudius' reign. After considering all of the sources, both biblical and extra-biblical, the fallible view and the infallible view will be weighed.

In the fourth chapter, the prophecy concerning Paul's imprisonment will be studied. Agabus' second prophecy will be dealt with in the same way the first prophecy is analyzed. Since this prophecy is very personal to Paul, his situation in Acts 21:10-14 must be properly understood. Along with the symbolic act of Agabus, important phrases and words such as τάδε λέγει τὸ πνεῦμα τὸ ἅγιον (Thus says the Holy Spirit), δήσουσιν (will bind), and παραδώσουσιν (will hand over) will be studied. To understand whether this prophecy was fulfilled, the subsequent narratives of Acts must be studied, especially the accounts of Paul in Jerusalem and his testimony in Acts 28:17. After considering all of these passages, and the three possible solutions for understanding the fulfillment of the prophecy, it will be seen whether Agabus' imprisonment prophecy is accurate.

In the fifth chapter, conclusions will be drawn concerning the foretelling accuracy of Agabus. After summarizing the discussion, implications for the church today will be briefly explained. It is hoped that this study will establish foretelling accuracy as an indispensable quality of NT prophecy.

# CHAPTER II

# VIEWS CONCERNING AGABUS' PROPHECIES

*Introduction*

It is important to become properly acquainted with the scholarly debate concerning the prophecies of Agabus. Though variously defined, NT prophecy can be regarded as either fallible or infallible in details. The fallible NT prophecy view will be studied first, followed by a study of the infallible NT prophecy view. For each view, the following topics will be covered (in no necessary order): 1) definition, 2) adherents, 3) relationship to OT prophecy, 4) NT support, and 5) specific views on Agabus.

## Fallible NT Prophecy View

One camp of scholars questions the accuracy and the authority of NT prophecy. This camp does not perceive NT prophecy as authoritative divine revelation in the tradition of the OT canonical prophecy or NT apostleship.

For the purpose of analyzing this camp, there are three tasks at hand. First, a basic definition will be offered. Then the view of Wayne Grudem will be considered. Lastly, contributions of other scholars will be surveyed.

*Basic Definition*

As the name suggests, the fallible NT prophecy view holds that NT prophecy is fallible in details. Whereas the canonical Scriptures are absolutely infallible and inspired, NT prophecy is susceptible to error. Thus, the utterance of a NT prophet must be carefully scrutinized, in order to distinguish between the divine accurate elements and the erroneous contents.

*Wayne Grudem' view*

Though several scholars represent the fallible NT prophecy camp, none has been as influential as Wayne Grudem. Grudem's influence and works make him the best representative of this camp.

*Influence of Grudem*

Wayne Grudem is perceived by many as the most popular adherent of the fallible NT prophecy view in the 19th-20th century. Critics note that Grudem found approval from the faculty of University of Cambridge and the leaders of "Third Wave" movements such as John Wimber.[18] *The Gift of Prophecy in the New Testament and Today* is cited as the justification for the prophetic activities in Kansas City Fellowship and Vineyard movements.[19]

The fact that Grudem's views have been noticed by the evangelical world is evident. Critics such as Kenneth

---

[18] With some modifications, Grudem's PhD dissertation at University of Cambridge was published as *The Gift of Prophecy in 1 Corinthians* in 1982. The more widely known work *The Gift of Prophecy in the New Testament and Today* was published six years later. David Oldham, "The Gift of Prophecy and Modern Revivals," *Reformation and Revival* 5:1 (1996) 112; Robert L. Thomas, "Prophecy Rediscovered? A Review of The Gift of Prophecy in the New Testament and Today," *BSac* 149 (1992) 83.

[19] Michael G. Maudlin, "Seers in the Heartland," *Christianity Today* 35 (January 14, 1991) 20.

Gentry opines that Grudem's *The Gift of Prophecy in the New Testament and Today* represents the best argument for this view and the book is endorsed by leading evangelical and Reformed scholars.[20] The ecumenical leader J.I. Packer has endorsed Grudem.[21] Also, according to Grudem, several scholars maintain that Grudem's view was 1) held by many Puritans such as Samuel Ruthford and Richard Baxter and 2) compatible with the Westminster Confession of faith.[22]

*Grudem's Definition*

So then one must turn to Grudem for the standard definition of the fallible NT prophecy view.[23] While pleading for a "middle ground" between cessationists and charismatics, Grudem presents NT prophecy as non-canonical rather than canonical, human rather than divine, and susceptible to error rather than infallible.[24] So

---

[20]Gentry cites the following theologians as supporters: J. I. Packer, Vern S. Poythress, Charles L. Holman, L. Russ Bush, Stanley Horton, H. Wayne House, and F. F. Bruce. Kenneth L. Gentry, Jr., *The*

*Charismatic Gift of Prophecy: A Reformed Response to Wayne Grudem* (Eugene, OR: Wipf & Stock, 2000) iii.

[21]Oldham, "The Gift of Prophecy and Modern Revivals," 112. On the back flap of the *The Gift of Prophecy in the New Testament and Today*, Packer writes: "Careful, thorough, wise, and to my mind, convincing."

[22]Wayne A. Grudem, *The Gift of Prophecy in the New Testament and Today* (Westchester, IL: Crossway Books, 2000) 13-14.

[23]However, Grudem himself does not present a lucid definition of NT prophecy. Farnell writes in a footnote: "Absence of an explicit definition makes an analysis of Grudem's work problematic." F. David Farnell, "Is the Gift of Prophecy for Today? Part 3: Does the New Testament Teach Two Prophetic Gifts?" *BSac* 150 (1993) 63. Thomas complains in a footnote: "One must piece together from scattered excerpts Grudem's concept of the gift." Thomas, "Prophecy Rediscovered?" 84.

[24]Grudem, *The Gift of Prophecy in the New Testament and Today*, 17-18. Grudem attempts to avoid the extreme positions of certain Charismatics such as Peter Wagner, who writes: "...God does speak today in a direct and specific way to particular needs and situations as He did among the ancient people of Israel and among

then, NT prophecies are not divine revelations on par with Scripture. Rather, these prophecies resemble hunches and can be vaguely defined as "a report of something that God brings to mind."[25] NT prophecy only has the authority of "mere human words," and is consequently susceptible to error and misinterpretation.[26]

### Grudem's View of the Prophet

Mistakes found in NT prophecy are explained by the disconnection between the NT prophets and their OT counterparts. Grudem asserts that the apostles are directly connected to the OT prophets, but NT prophets are not.[27] So then, corresponding to the two offices of the apostle and the prophet, there are now two strands of prophecy, one called "apostolic" prophecy and the other called "ordinary congregational prophecy."[28] The former is authoritative but does not exist anymore because the canon is closed. The latter still exists, albeit without absolute divine authority.

### Arguments from 1 Corinthians

The most substantial and fundamental arguments for Grudem's view come from five verses or passages of 1 Corinthians.[29] First, he devotes considerable attention to

---

Christians in the first century." C. Peter Wagner, *Your Spiritual Gifts Can Help Your Church Grow* (Glendale: G/L Regal Books, 1976) 228.

[25]Ibid., 18. See also, Wayne A. Grudem, *Systematic Theology* (Grand Rapids: Zondervan, 1994) 1049.

[26]Grudem, *The Gift of Prophecy in the New Testament and Today*, 69.

[27]Ibid., 27.

[28] Perhaps influenced by the criticisms of Max Turner and D. A. Carson (to be observed later), Grudem is wary of presenting two types of prophecies. He says the NT prophecy and apostolic prophecies are not different in "kind," but in level of authority. Ibid., 47-49, 90.

[29]Actually, Grudem mentions six verses or short passages, but he groups 1 Cor 11:5 and 1 Cor 14:34-35 together for the purpose of one argument. The other four arguments come from 1 Cor 14:29, 30, 36, and 37-38. Ibid., 69.

an analysis of 1 Cor 14:29. He defines two important words in that verse that shape his whole outlook of NT prophecy: οἱ ἄλλοι and διακρίνω. Concerning the first word, Grudem believes it refers to the whole congregation, not other prophets or those with the gift of discernment.[30] The entire congregation can and should be judging uttered prophecy.[31]

How the second word διακρίνω (judge) is understood is extremely crucial to Grudem's argument. First he divorces this word from its noun form (διακρίσις). He writes:

> But it must be noted that both the noun and the verb have a wide range of meaning. It is not at all unlikely that Paul would have used *diakrisis* in 1 Corinthians 12:10 to mean "distinguishing" (among different kinds of spirits) while using *diakrinō* in 14:29 to mean something quite different, such as "evaluate" or "judge" (prophetic utterances). In fact, in 1 Corinthians alone Paul uses the verb *diakrinō* in several senses.[32]

So "judge" in 1 Cor 14:29 is not to be defined as a strict act of rejection or acceptance of *"spirits"* that enter the believing community, but rather a sifting of *prophetic content.* Grudem thinks that if a harsh standard is intended here, Paul would have employed κρίνω, which is a stricter legal term.[33] A more lenient act of "evaluating" (διακρίνω) is much more appropriate for

---

[30]Ibid., 54-57. See also E. Earle Ellis, "Prophecy in the New Testament Church—and Today," *Prophetic Vocation in the New Testament and Today* (Ed. J. Panagopoulos; Supplement to Novum Testamentum, Vol XLV; Leiden: E. J. Brill, 1977) 52.

[31]Grudem, *The Gift of Prophecy in the New Testament and Today*, 57.

[32]Ibid., 54.

[33]Ibid., 60.

prophets who do not have authority of apostles or OT prophets. Every member of the congregation would distinguish "good from the less good, what was thought to be helpful from the unhelpful, what was perceived to be true from the false."[34]

The second argument of Grudem in 1 Corinthians comes from 1 Cor 14:30. From this verse one can conclude that it is tolerable to interrupt a NT prophet when another person has a more urgent revelation. According to Grudem, Paul is "totally unconcerned" about such prophetic utterances being lost forever.[35] If God's words were being spoken through a prophet to the church, should Paul not show more effort to preserve the words?[36] In Grudem's mind, this practice of interruption is approved by Paul. In this manner, Paul endorsed the view that prophets lack authority.

The next two arguments can be grouped together. In 1 Cor 14:36-38, Paul directly subjugates the NT prophets to apostolic authority in two ways. First, Paul asks a rhetorical question to imply that the word of God does not originate from prophets (1 Cor 14:36). Grudem perceives that Paul makes this statement because the authority of the NT prophets is without divine authority.[37] Then in 1 Cor 14:37-38, Paul asserts his authority by claiming his words to be "a command of the Lord."[38] A NT prophet could not claim the same authority.

Grudem's last argument from 1 Corinthians concerns the women's practice of prophecy. An apparent tension between 1 Cor 11:5 and 1 Cor 14:34 exists due to the

---

[34]Ibid.
[35]Ibid., 62.
[36]Ibid., 62-63.
[37]Ibid., 66-67.
[38]Ibid., 68-69.

liberty of speech given to the women prophets in the congregation in the former verse, and the command to remain silent in the latter. However, Grudem believes his definition of prophecy can be used to reconcile the two verses. The type of speech that is forbidden in 1 Cor 14:34 is speech with authority over men.[39] However, in 1 Cor 11:5, women are permitted to prophesy, which implies that the act of prophecy was not divinely authoritative.[40] Unlike teaching and preaching, women can practice the NT prophetic gift because it does not carry divine authority.

Grudem's exegesis of 1 Corinthians is the *crux interpretum* of his work. He establishes five arguments. First and foremost, NT prophecy is sifted without rejecting the prophet (1 Cor 14:29). Secondly, Paul is not concerned about prophecy being lost (1 Cor 14:30). Thirdly, Paul implies that the word of God does not originate from prophets (1 Cor 14:36). Fourth, Paul subjugates the NT prophet under his authority (1 Cor 14:37-38). Lastly, Paul allows women to prophecy in the congregation with men because prophecy is not divinely authoritative like teaching and preaching (1 Cor 11:5; 1 Cor 14:34).

### Views Concerning Agabus

As a result of the conclusions above, NT prophets like Agabus are relegated to a non-authoritative status or branded as poor transmitters of divine revelation. Prophecies of Agabus in Acts 11:28 and in 21:10-11 lack divine authority and are prone to mistakes. Grudem observes that in Acts 11:28, διὰ τοῦ πνεύματος (through the Spirit) indicates a "loose relationship between the Holy Spirit and the prophet."[41] Also, "a degree of

---

[39] Ibid., 68.
[40] Ibid., 68-69.
[41] Ibid., 71-72.

imprecision" accompanies the word "indicate" (ἐσήμανεν), which explains the error of Agabus.[42]

In Acts 21:10-11, at least two alleged errors are found. First, it was not the Jews who eventually bound Paul at Jerusalem as Agabus predicted, but the Romans (Acts 21:33; 22:29).[43] Secondly, Jews did not deliver Paul into the hands of Romans, but out of zeal attempted to take his life.[44] Grudem writes concerning the word "deliver" (παραδίδωμι): "Essential to the sense of this word is the idea of actively, consciously, willingly 'delivering, giving over, handing over' something or someone to someone (or something) else—this is the case in all of the other 119 instances of its use in the New Testament."[45]

So then, when compared with prophecies of OT and Lukan writings, Agabus does not meet the standard of accuracy, but he does meet the standards of 1 Corinthians 14.[46] In Grudem's theory, Agabus amalgamates divine revelation with his own interpretation that contained mistakes.[47] Luke recorded both this prophecy and the account of Paul in Acts that shows how Agabus was wrong on details.[48]

*Summary*

In conclusion, Grudem argues that Agabus is a prime example of NT prophets whose authority is not as absolute as the apostles or the prophets of OT. The majority of support for this view comes from 1

---

[42]Ibid., 72.
[43]Ibid., 78.
[44]Ibid.
[45]Ibid.
[46]Ibid., 79-80.
[47]Ibid., 81.
[48]Ibid.

Corinthians and Acts, where NT prophets are viewed as capable of mistakes in the transmission of revelation.

*Major Supporters of Grudem's View*

According to Richard Gaffin, other major scholars that have similar or identical views as Grudem are D. A. Carson, Roy Clements, Graham Houston, and Max Turner.[49] Sam Storms, in recent decade have also contributed much to Grudem's camp. With the exception of Clements, these scholars are still influential today, serving in influential schools or ministry positions.[50] Though their treatments of the issue are not as exhaustive as Grudem's, these scholars generally tend to demote NT prophecy under apostolic prophecy. Some of them also provide insights that Grudem integrates. The contributions of Turner, Carson, Houston, Storms will be observed.

*Max Turner*

Max Turner's publication in *Vox Evangelica* has striking affinity to Grudem's treatise. Turner views a NT prophetic oracle as parallel to a mixture of wheat and chaff which must be distinguished (διακρίνω) (1 Cor 14:29).[51] Turner explicitly writes concerning Grudem:

---

[49]Richard B. Gaffin Jr., "A Cessationist View," *Are Miraculous Gifts for Today? Four Views* (Counterpoints; Ed. Wayne A. Grudem; Grand Rapids, MI: Zondervan, 1996) 48.

[50]In 1999, Clements, a former member of the British Evangelical Alliance management team and the pastor of Eden Baptist Church in Cambridge, resigned from his pastoral post to pursue a homosexual lifestyle. "Evangelical Leader Leaves Wife for Man." *Christianity Today* 43 (November 15, 1999) 29.

[51]"The presupposition is that any one New Testament prophetic oracle is expected to be mixed in quality, and the wheat must be separated from the chaff. The prophet may genuinely have received something from God (albeit often indistinctly), but the 'vision' is partial, limited in perspective, and prone to wrong interpretation by the prophet even as he declares it (1 Cor. 13:12)." Max Turner, "Spiritual Gifts Then and Now," *Vox Evangelica* 15 (1985) 16.

"We fully accept that he has put his finger on an important issue, and that Paul does relativize the authority of prophetic communication in the church."[52]

However, Turner is not convinced that one can make sharp distinctions between the NT prophets and the apostles. All prophecies are only partially understood. He prefers to use the term "spectrum of authority":

> And this suggests, what seems reasonable on other grounds too, namely, that there was no sharp distinction between apostolic prophecy and prophets' prophesyings—rather, a spectrum of authority of charisma extending from apostolic speech and prophecy (backed by apostolic commission) at one extreme, to vague and barely profitable attempts at oracular speech such as brought 'prophecy' as a whole into question at Thessalonika (1 Thess 5:19f) at the other. A prophet's speech might fall anywhere on the spectrum, so the task of evaluation fell on the congregation.[53]

Though his distinction between apostolic prophecy and the prophecies of the NT prophecies are not as pronounced as Grudem's, Turner nonetheless sees a hierarchy of authority. In other words, while his exegesis of 1 Cor 13:12 leads him to conclude that apostolic prophecy is partial (ἐκ μέρους) as much as the prophecy of NT prophets, he still attributes lesser authority to the latter based on 1 Cor 14.[54] Evaluation is needed to

---

[52]Ibid.

[53]Ibid.

[54]Ibid. Turner writes later: "Indeed, although Paul's wording in Ephesians 2:20, and his ranking of prophets second only to apostles in 1 Corinthians 12:28, suggest that the prophetic word of some established prophets contributed to the laying down of precedents, norms and traditions in the church (an activity which ultimately marginalized the prophets), Paul nevertheless clearly subordinates the authority of the

distinguish between the false elements and the true elements of NT prophecies.

### D. A. Carson

D. A. Carson also expresses his view in his work on 1 Cor 12-14. He accepts and adapts the propositions of Grudem and Turner before him. For example, his view on 1 Cor 14:29 is the same as Turner's.[55] Also, Carson is "generally sympathetic" to the view of Grudem.[56] In fact, Carson summarizes and incorporates the arguments of Grudem, with some refinement.[57] His conclusions concerning Agabus are quite negative:

> The prophecy of Agabus in Acts 21:10-11 stipulates that the Jews at Jerusalem would bind the man who owns Paul's girdle and hand him over to the Gentiles. Strictly speaking, however, in the event itself, Paul was not bound by the Jews but by the Romans; and the Jews did not hand Paul over to the Romans, but sought to kill him with mob violence, prompting a rescue by the Romans. I can think of no reported Old Testament prophet whose prophecies are so wrong on the details.[58]

Carson does have two minor reservations concerning Grudem's arguments. He writes, "My

---

prophetic phenomena at Corinth to his own (cf. 14:37ff.). He does not feel able to allow the Corinthian prophets to decide the agenda for worship, but specifies *how* they are to operate, and further relativizes their authority by demanding congregational sifting of their utterances. It would seem that Paul did not regard the Corinthian practice of the revelatory gifts, which he describes in 1 Corinthians 12:8-10, as of primary significance in the shaping of theological structures." Ibid., 54.

[55]Carson, *Showing the Spirit*, 94-95; Turner, "Spiritual Gifts Then and Now," 16.

[56]Carson, *Showing the Spirit*, 94.

[57]Ibid., 94-100.

[58]Ibid., 97-98.

hesitations about this thesis are two, neither of which does irreparable damage to it, but only refines it."[59] First, Carson allows two kinds of prophecy in OT as well as NT.[60] Secondly, Carson, like Turner, is not satisfied with Grudem's sharp distinction between apostolic prophecy and the prophecy of the NT prophets.[61]

*Graham Houston*

From University of Aberdeen came Graham Houston whose work also supports Grudem. Houston studied under I. Howard Marshall, and the years of study on the topic of NT prophecy resulted in his work *Prophecy: A Gift for Today?*[62] The release of this book demonstrates that the controversy of the NT prophecy is a concern among scholars in Europe as well as America. Also, Houston's pastoral influence brings the controversy beyond the bounds of the scholarly field. In his book, Houston essentially agrees with Grudem:

> To summarize: the apostles were so designated because they were the authoritative messengers, commissioned by the risen Christ (1 Cor 9:1), who proclaimed the word of the Lord in the same way as the canonical prophets of Old Testament fame. Those called 'prophets' in the New Testament churches were not comparable in authority and function to classical Old Testament prophets, but were

---

[59]Ibid., 98.

[60]Ibid. This bifurcation of OT prophecy is expounded by Graham Houston. Graham Houston, *Prophecy: A Gift for Today?* (Downers Grove, IL: InterVarsity Press, 1989) 38.

[61]Carson, *Showing the Spirit*, 98-99.

[62]I. Howard Marshall contributes to Houston's work by writing the foreword. In it he comments that Aberdeen has attracted some important "students of prophecy." Houston is the NT counterpart to Joel B. Green, who specializes in OT prophecy. Houston, *Prophecy: A Gift for Today?*, 9-10.

subject to the authority of the message proclaimed by the apostles.[63]

However, Houston differs from Grudem in his approach to OT prophecy. Whereas Grudem generalizes OT prophecy to be completely authoritative without exception, Houston avers that there were at least two types of prophecy in the OT. He writes that one type communicated God's word with "absolute verbal authority," while another type was experienced as "a powerful sign of God's presence without necessarily bringing a specific message."[64] In spite of this difference with Grudem, Houston arrives at the same conclusions concerning Agabus' utterances. The non-authoritative type of prophecy seen in OT is exemplified in Agabus' prophecies.[65]

*Sam Storms*

The senior pastor of Bridgeway Church in Oklahoma City has an impressive list of credentials: founder of Enjoying God Ministries, former professor, author of over two dozen books, popular blogger, four decades of ministry, and president of Evangelical Theological Society. Needless to say, his influence is palpable. Storms communicates a Reformed Charismatic position to pastors in the same way Wayne Grudem did for theologians. His book, *Practicing the Power: Welcoming the Gifts of the Holy Spirit in Your Life*, dedicated to Grudem, primes church leaders for the full use of spiritual gifts in their congregations. In the work, Storms offers plenty of warning and practical advice. For example, a person who tries to experiment with Storms'

---

[63] Ibid., 73-74.
[64] Ibid., 38.
[65] Ibid., 61-63.

ideas may suffer loss in attendance.[66] Also, a sample prayer for spiritual gifts is provided as a template.[67]

Due to its importance, Storms devotes three chapters to the topic of prophecy.[68] He warns against its confusion with enlightenment, illumination, and other forms of Spirit-enablement. Prophecy is "the human report of a divine revelation" that involves disclosure of knowledge unobtainable through natural means.[69]

Acts 21:1-36, which describes the plight of Paul, is the key paradigmatic passage for prophetic practice.[70] Every prophecy is composed of revelation, interpretation, and application. The believers in Tyre and Caesarea receive the same revelation about dangers ahead for Paul and interpret it correctly but disagree on the application.[71] These diverse conclusions take place under the heading of "prophecy." As for Agabus, his mistake was not the application, but interpretation of the vision he received. His prophecy, mixed with truth and error, predicts that Jews will bind Paul and hand him to the Gentiles (Acts 21:11). Paul, however, was not bound by Jews and they did not deliver him consciously to the Romans.[72] In Acts 28:17, Paul describes not the mob scene in the Temple, but his transfer to Caesarea (23:12-35).[73]

---

[66] Sam Storms, *Practicing the Power: Welcoming the Gifts of the Holy Spirit in Your Life* (Grand Rapids: Zondervan, 2017) 29.
[67] Ibid., 39.
[68] Ibid., 146.
[69] Ibid., 82, 96.
[70] Ibid., 104.
[71] Ibid., 113-15.
[72] Ibid., 116-17.
[73] Ibid., 117-18.

Such combination of mistakes and genuine revelation is typical, so church leaders ought to promote prophetic ministry, as long as they cultivate "prophetic humility."[74] Beginners may start in small groups, since they best emulate the early church house churches.[75] Storms stresses the importance of prophecy in the church accompanied by discernment and accepting failed prophecies.[76]

*Summary*

The fallible NT prophecy view defines NT prophecy as a mixture of God's revelation and human error. Grudem is the most influential proponent of this view and bases his arguments largely on 1 Corinthians. Based on the arguments of the epistle, Agabus' prophecies are perceived as non-authoritative and laden with mistakes. Other supporters of Grudem either support or modify his view slightly.

## Infallible NT Prophecy View

Another camp of scholars rejects the notion that the gift of prophecy is fallible. In fact, NT prophets not only receive revelation, but deliver the message without adding any mistakes. Evidence for this view will be outlined and implications for Agabus will be explored.

*Basic Definition*

The infallible NT prophecy view holds that NT prophecy is infallible in details. NT prophecy, like the canonical Scriptures, is absolutely inspired and infallible in content. The prophet not only receives the authoritative message, but also delivers it without appending any

---

[74] Ibid., 119.
[75] Ibid., 124-25.
[76] Ibid., 189-91. 1

errors. NT prophecy is seen as mistake-free in content, both during reception and during delivery of the message.

*Major Opponents of Grudem's view*

A plethora of scholars from various fronts have either reacted against Grudem's fallible NT prophecy view summarized above or unequivocally maintained the infallible view of prophecy. Notable names include John F. Walvoord, Herman Bavinck, Louis Berkhof, John Murray, Benjamin B. Warfield, F. F. Bruce, Leon Morris, and W. E. Vine.[77] The great number of scholars in this camp suggests that this view is the more traditional view. Since it is difficult to list them all, the most suitable representatives will be noted. Two scholars have made notable contributions recently: Richard B. Gaffin Jr. and F. David Farnell.[78]

---

[77] John F. Walvoord, *Holy Spirit: A Comprehensive Study of the Person and Work of the Holy Spirit* (Wheaton: Van Kampen Press, 1954) 177-78. Gentry provides an extensive list of 33 Reformed scholars and 19 evangelical scholars who argue for the infallible view of NT prophecy. He also includes relevant quotes from each of them. Gentry, *The Charismatic Gift of Prophecy*, 75-107.

[78] Kenneth L. Gentry Jr. can be mentioned here as well. His arguments frequently overlap with those of Gaffin and Farnell. For example, he stresses the reinitiation of ancient prophecy in the day of Pentecost and the foundational authority of the NT prophet like Farnell and Gaffin. However, Gentry contributes to the infallible NT prophecy view in various other ways: 1) lexical studies of "prophecy," "revelation," and "mystery," lend support to the view that prophetic utterances are divinely inspired; 2) a survey of reformed and evangelical opinion provides historical support; 3) the influential writings of John Calvin, Westminster Confession, and the Presbyterian Church of America cannot be used to advance the fallible NT prophecy view; 4) one must be wary of theological implications that allow an "open canon"; and 5) The book of Revelation cannot be readily used to support the fallible NT prophecy view. Kenneth L. Gentry, Jr., *The Charismatic Gift of Prophecy: A Reformed Response to Wayne Grudem* (Eugene, OR: Wipf & Stock, 2000).

*Richard B. Gaffin Jr.*

The importance of Richard Gaffin Jr. in this debate is clearly demonstrated in Grudem's frequent responses to him. Gaffin is mentioned often both in the main pages and the endnotes of Grudem's *The Gift of Prophecy in the New Testament and Today*. In fact, no other scholar is mentioned more. Elsewhere, Grudem considers Gaffin a suitable representative of the cessationist position.[79] So then, it is appropriate to summarize Gaffin's view.

Gaffin presents five major rejoinders against the fallible NT prophecy view. To begin, all NT prophets are, without distinction, foundational to the church just as the apostles were (Eph 2:20; 3:5).[80] Grudem's argument that τῶν ἀποστόλων καὶ προφητῶν refer to apostles who are prophets is tenuous, being without grammatical support.[81] He appears to yield to Gaffin's arguments on the topic of Eph 2:20.[82]

Secondly, Agabus' prophecies in Acts do not support the fallible NT prophecy view. In Acts 21:10-11, as in Acts

---

[79]Grudem, "Preface," 14.

[80]Richard B. Gaffin Jr., "A Cessationist View," *Are Miraculous Gifts for Today? Four Views* (Ed. Wayne A. Grudem; Grand Rapids, MI: Zondervan, 1996) 48-49.

[81]Ibid., 48.

[82]Grudem admits, "Gaffin's discussion on pages 93-102 is the most careful statement of the position that Eph 2:20 applies to all prophets in the New Testament churches and shows that the gift of prophecy has ceased." Grudem, *The Gift of Prophecy in the New Testament and Today*, 364. Richard B. Gaffin, Jr., "Prophecy and Tongues," *Perspectives on Pentecost* (Phillipsburg, NJ: Presbyterian and Reformed, 1979) 93-102. However, it is difficult to determine how important the passages from Ephesians are to Grudem and his arguments. On the one hand, one can agree with R. Fowler White that length of Grudem's discussion on verses from Ephesians reveals its importance. R. Fowler White, "Gaffin and Grudem on Eph 2:20: In Defense of Gaffin's Exegesis," *WTJ* 54 (1992) 303. On the other hand, one must note that Grudem consigns his discussions of Eph 2:20 and 3:5 from an early chapter to an appendix in his 2000 edition. Grudem, *The Gift of Prophecy in the New Testament and Today*, 329-46.

21:4, Paul appears to defy the pleadings of the congregation to stop his journey to Jerusalem. However, such pleas must not be confused as the authoritative, infallible prophetic word. Opinions and revelations are fundamentally distinct. Gaffin writes concerning Acts 21:4 and Acts 21:10-11:

> Both these instances, in turn, illustrate the sweeping truth expressed earlier by Paul himself in giving the Ephesian elders an overall account of his unique ministry: "I only know that in *every* city *the Holy Spirit* warns me that prison and hardships are facing me." (Acts 20:23). The fact that on both occasions disciples (perhaps even Agabus himself and others who prophesied) sought to dissuade Paul in no way compromises the Spirit-breathed, infallible truthfulness of what was prophesied. Also, if Agabus made errors, that apparently was lost on Luke. There is no indication that he records this incident other than as it serves his overarching purpose to show the advance of the gospel from Jerusalem to Rome.[83]

The third argument of Gaffin relates to 1 Corinthians. The word diakri,nw in 1 Cor 14:29 has a variety of senses and should not be limited to a sifting process between human error and authoritative prophecy.[84] Also, 1 Cor 14:36a is not a convincing proof text for the fallible NT prophecy view, because Paul's question in that verse addresses the whole church and is not exclusive to the prophets.[85] Finally, 1 Cor 14:37-38 and the rest of 1 Cor 14 concern *conduct* of prophets more than the prophetic *content*.[86] So once the key texts

---

[83]Gaffin Jr., "A Cessationist View," 49-50.
[84]Ibid., 50.
[85]Ibid.
[86]Ibid.

from 1 Cor 14 are reassessed, not much support for the fallible NT prophecy view remains.

The fourth argument concerns the ranking of spiritual gifts in 1 Cor 12:28. It is clear from that verse that Paul ranks the prophetic gift second only to the apostolic gift in terms of usefulness.[87] However, Grudem diminishes the value of the prophetic gift to the point where even clear biblical teaching exceeds it in worth. Gaffin finds preposterous the inevitable conclusion that follows:

> If so, then their view is left with the following conclusion: In the church prophecy, always subject to evaluation as fallible and therefore never binding on anyone, is more useful and edifying than teaching based on God's clear, authoritative, and inerrant word! Prophecy takes precedence over such teaching! An obviously unwanted and unacceptable conclusion, I would hope. But how can they avoid this conclusion?[88]

The fifth argument presented by Gaffin is a concern for the sufficiency of canonical Scripture which is undermined through Grudem's view of prophecy. Though the fallible NT prophecy view distinguishes between the gift and the Scriptures, the spontaneous utterances are bound to receive more attention from the church. He writes:

> This view, I cannot see otherwise, opens the door to revelation in the life of the church today that is neither (inscripturated) special, redemptive revelation nor general revelation (from ourselves, as created in God's image, and

---

[87]Grudem, *The Gift of Prophecy in the New Testament and Today,* 52-53.
[88]Gaffin Jr., "A Cessationist View," 51.

the world about us). What is affirmed is a *third kind of revelation* that goes beyond both. It is more than "revelation" in the sense of the Spirit's illumination for today of already revealed truth (Eph. 1:17; Phil. 3:15), more than thoughtful reflection and prayerful wrestling, prompted by the Spirit, about contemporary circumstances and problems in the light of Scripture. In view is additional, immediate revelation that functions, especially where guidance is concerned, beyond Scripture and so unavoidably implies a certain insufficiency in Scripture that needs to be compensated for. The tendency of this view, no matter how carefully it is qualified, is to divert attention from Scripture, particularly in practical and pressing life issues.[89]

Thus, in conclusion, Gaffin expresses his disfavor with the fallible NT prophecy view in five arguments. First, prophets are foundational to the church just as the apostles are. Secondly, Agabus is a prophet who keeps truth separate from his opinions. Thirdly, 1 Corinthians 14 teaches the proper conduct of the NT prophecy without specific insight into its content. Fourthly, it is difficult to uphold that the prophetic gift, ranked only second to the apostolic gift can be less reliable than clear teaching from the Scriptures. Lastly, sufficiency of Scriptures is compromised if prophecy exists outside the bounds of special revelation or general revelation.

*F. David Farnell*

Grudem identifies two dispensationist schools that hold the cessationist view: Dallas Theological Seminary and Master's Seminary.[90] From the latter, F. David Farnell

---

[89] Ibid., 52.
[90] Grudem, "Preface," 10.

emerged as a vocal opponent, especially against Grudem's view of prophecy. Farnell's four-part series entitled "Is the Gift of Prophecy for Today?" in *Bibliotheca Sacra* is suggested by one scholar as the future "standard cessationist treatment of the gift of prophecy."[91] With such praise attributed to this work, a summary of Farnell is appropriate here.[92]

The first article of Farnell places the current debate concerning the NT prophetic gift in its proper historical context. In other words, Grudem's call for compromise between the cessationist and the non-cessationist views is indeed a modern concern, but requires a historical survey.[93] Especially relevant is the period between the first and second century. In the latter half of the first century, the infestation of false prophecy in Asia leads to stern warnings and sharp rebukes against them (1 John 4:1-3; Rev 2:12-17, 20; 22:18-19).[94] Later, the writers of the *Didache* and the *Shepherd of Hermas* equip the church against false prophets with litmus tests of behavior and motives.[95] However, no false prophecy was as controversial as the one sourced in Montanism. With numerous departures from the biblical truth and conduct, especially the OT standard, Montanists were condemned and prophetic fervor abated until the present era.[96]

---

[91] Myron J. Houghton, "A Reexamination of 1 Corinthians 13:8-13," *BSac* 153 (1996) 346.

[92] Like Grudem, Farnell began the formulation of his ideas with his Ph.D. dissertation. See F. David Farnell, "The New Testament Prophetic Gift: Its Nature and Duration," (Ph.D. dissertation, Dallas Theological Seminary, Dallas, Texas, 1990).

[93] Farnell, "Is the Gift of Prophecy for Today? Part 1: The Current Debate about New Testament Prophecy," 280-82.

[94] Ibid., 282-84.

[95] Ibid., 284-88.

[96] Ibid., 289-95. See Chapter I for information concerning the present interest in NT prophecy.

The second article of Farnell argues for a firm connection between the NT prophets and the OT prophets, established on the day of Pentecost. Between the testaments, canonical prophets were absent, though many were fervent for a return of the prophetic gift promised in Joel 2:28-32.[97] Peter not only confirms the renewal of the Spirit in the manner of Joel's prediction, he emphasizes the gift of prophecy that is revived.[98] The same Spirit that is known by the OT prophets manifests Himself among the NT prophets. Thus, the emergence of figures such as Agabus and John the Apostle, who act and speak like OT prophets is not coincidental.[99] Farnell writes concerning Agabus:

> The continuity between Old Testament and New Testament prophecy is also demonstrated by Agabus. Agabus modeled his prophetic style directly after the Old Testament prophets...This can be seen in several ways. He introduced his prophecy with the formula, "This is what the Holy Spirit says" (Τάδε λέγει τὸ πνεῦμα τὸ ἅγιον, Acts 21:11), which closely parallels the Old Testament prophetic formula of "thus says the Lord" so frequently proclaimed by Old Testament prophets (e.g., Isa 7:7; Ezek 5:5; Amos 1:3, 6, 11, 13; Obad 1; Mic 2:3; Nah 1:12; Zech 1:3-4). This same introductory phrase introduces the word of the Lord Jesus to the seven churches in the Book of Revelation (τάδε λέγει, cf. Rev 2:1, 8, 12, 18;

---

[97] David F. Farnell, "Is the Gift of Prophecy for Today? Part 2: The Gift of Prophecy in the Old and New Testaments," *BSac* 149 (1992) 388-91. For a discussion of apocalyptic literature that arose during the intertestamental times, see Charles F. Pfeiffer, *Between the Testaments* (Grand Rapids: Baker, 1959) 121-24; Aune, *Prophecy*, 103-05.

[98] This emphasis is indicated by Peter's commentary to Joel 2:28 in Acts 2:18, "and they will prophesy" (kai. profhteu,sousin). Ibid., 391-93.

[99] Ibid., 393-99.

3:1, 7, 14). Like many Old Testament prophets, Agabus presented his prophecies through symbolic actions (Acts 21:11; cf. 1 Kings 11:29-40; 22:11; Isa 20:1-6; Jer 13:1-11; Ezek 4:1-17; 5:1-17). Like the Old Testament prophets, Agabus was empowered by the Holy Spirit as the prophetic messenger (διὰ τοῦ πνεύματος, Acts 11:28; cf. Num 11:25-29; 1 Sam 10:6, 10; 2 Sam 23:2; Isa 42:1; 59:21; Zech 7:12; Neh 9:30). Like the Old Testament prophets, Agabus's prophecies were accurately fulfilled (Acts 11:27-28; 21:10-11; cf. 28:17).[100]

In addition, the epistles of the NT also show OT connection. Farnell believes the evaluation in the Corinthian assembly is the same type of evaluation that takes place in Israel, with a severe penalty for failure (Deut 13:1-13; 18:20-22).[101] A true Christian prophet withstands this sort of evaluation because he or she is empowered by the same Spirit that empowered the OT prophets.[102] Finally, a proper exegesis of Eph 2:20 reaffirms the NT prophet as a co-authoritative channel of revelation along with the apostle.[103]

The third article of Farnell is a critical work focusing on Grudem's presentation of two types of NT prophecy. Thus, it deserves special attention. First, Farnell discusses Grudem's influence and his definition.[104] Then he argues for the continuity of prophecy from OT to NT. As seen in

---

[100]Ibid., 395-96.

[101]Ibid., 399-404.

[102]Ibid., 404-06.

[103]Ibid., 406-10. When one compares Gaffin and Farnell, it appears that the former emphasizes the prophet's equal authority with the apostles, while the latter emphasizes the connection between the NT prophet and the OT prophet.

[104]Farnell, "Is the Gift of Prophecy for Today? Part 3: Does the New Testament Teach Two Prophetic Gifts?" 62-65.

the *Didache* and the various documents that dealt with the Montanist controversy, the standards used to judge prophets in the post-apostolic church are the same as the OT standards.[105] NT prophets are judged by OT standards.

Two more major criticisms of Grudem follow. One major mistake of Grudem is a grammatical misapplication of the Granville-Sharp rule. The rule does not permit two plural nouns to be equated as one, as with "apostles-prophets" (Eph 2:20).[106] Also, Grudem does not recognize the NT evidence for the prestige enjoyed by the NT prophets (1 Cor 12:28; 14:1; Eph 2:20; 3:5).[107] NT prophets are just as authoritative as the apostles.

Later, Farnell argues for a balanced view of the prophetic office, whether it is from the OT or the NT. On the one hand, NT prophets must not be undermined. Since the prophetic potency was far more widespread in the church community than the OT community, Paul had to guard against abuses, which he does in 1 Cor 14:29-31.[108] There is no need to infer from this situation that NT prophets are lacking authority. On the other hand, one should not be naïve in understanding OT prophets in Israelite history. The OT prophets are overly idealized in Grudem's mind since he does not account that they too were disobeyed, different in popularity, persecuted, and

---

[105] Ibid., 66-70.

[106] Ibid., 73-79. Granville-Sharp writes: "...there is no exception, that I know of, which necessarily requires a construction different from what is there laid down, EXCEPT the nouns be *proper names*, or in the plural number; in which case there are many exceptions..." Granville Sharp, *Remarks on the Uses of the Definite Article in the Greek Text of the New Testament: Containing Many New Proofs of the Divinity of Christ, from Passages which are wrongly Translated in the Common English Version* (1st American ed; from the 3rd London ed.; Philadelphia: Hopkins, 1807) 6. See also Daniel A. Wallace, "The Article-Noun-*kai*-Noun Plural Construction," GTJ 4 (1983) 59-84.

[107] Ibid., 79-80.

[108] Ibid., 81.

evaluated firmly.[109] If the strict environment and popularity are indicators of authority, OT prophets must be questioned along with the NT prophets.

Farnell completes his third article with some reevaluation of 1 Cor 14. The ones who evaluate the NT prophets (οἱ ἄλλοι) are not comprised of the whole congregation, but should be equated with other prophets (1 Cor 14:29).[110] Also, the interruption of NT prophecy does not imply inferiority, but simply a rational control over expression (1 Cor 14:30-32).[111] Finally, Paul does not subject the NT prophets to a lower position than apostles because the content of their prophecy was inferior, but because false teachings were entering the church at a regular rate.[112] A new teaching must always be checked against an older teaching.

The fourth article of Farnell concentrates on the duration of the prophetic gift. In this article, the miraculous nature of NT prophecy is supported by 1) its divine source, 2) its revelatory, often-predictive function (which can also serve to comfort, encourage and exhort), and 3) the mediation of the Spirit.[113] Consequently, the

---

[109] Ibid., 81-83.

[110] Ibid., 83-85.

[111] Ibid., 85-86.

[112] Ibid., 87.

[113] F. David Farnell, "Is the Gift of Prophecy for Today? Part 4: When Will the Gift of Prophecy Cease?" *BSac* 150 (1993) 171-82. Farnell ponders whether prediction, alongside revelation, is an essential part of NT prophecy. He tends to exclude prediction as an indispensable part of the gift, based on exegesis of several passages. All of the following passages are prophetic without being predictive: Gentile inclusion in the church (Eph 3:5-10); the gospel of Christ and justification by faith (Acts 9:3-6, 20; Gal 1:12; 16-17); designation of Barnabas and Saul as missionaries (Acts 13:1-3); supernatural discernment (Matt 26:67-68; Mark 14:65; Luke 22:64); insight into personal life and character (Luke 7:39; John 4:19; 1 Cor 14:29-31). Ibid., 175-76. For an opposing view, see Edgar and Thomas. Thomas R. Edgar *Miraculous Gifts: Are They for Today?* (Neptune, NJ: Loizeaux Brothers, 1983) 72; Thomas, "Prophecy Rediscovered?" 94.

miraculous nature of the gift distinguishes the prophet from the teacher, the preacher, the evangelist, and the possessor of knowledge.[114]

Duration of the gift, the central focus of the fourth article, is the last topic. The bulk of arguments for cessation of the prophetic gift come from Eph 2:20 and 1 Cor 13:10, which state that prophets are primarily foundational as the apostles were and that the maturity (τὸ τέλειον) already reached by the church precludes the need for the gift, respectively.[115] Since the OT standard of accuracy prevails today and certain periods of history witnessed cessation of revelatory gifts, the best conclusion concerning NT prophecy is that the gift has ceased.[116]

In conclusion, Farnell supports the infallible NT prophecy view. First of all, the question concerning the authority of the NT prophet is not a new one. Secondly, the NT prophet is connected to the OT prophets. Thirdly, the arguments presented by Grudem fall short on many levels. Fourthly, there is ample evidence that the gift of prophecy ceased.

*Summary*

Some notable exegetical arguments are employed to refute the views of the fallible NT prophecy view. Gaffin and Farnell both uphold the authority of the NT prophet, albeit with different starting points. It can be asserted that the foundational passage for Gaffin is Eph 2:20, while the foundational passage for Farnell is Deut 18:20-22.[117] In these approaches, NT prophets such as

---

[114]Farnell, "Is the Gift of Prophecy for Today? Part 4: When Will the Gift of Prophecy Cease?" 182-85.

[115]Ibid., 185-95.

[116]Ibid., 196-202.

[117]For further discussion on the relationship between NT prophecy and OT prophecy, see John W. Hilber, "Diversity of OT Prophetic Phenomena and NT Prophecy," *WTJ* 56 (1994) 243-58.

Agabus are placed on equal stance with the apostles and their OT counterparts, respectively. Thus, in this view, Agabus is not a fallible prophet.

## Conclusion

Both the fallible NT prophecy view and the infallible NT prophecy view claim biblical support for their arguments. Grudem bases his arguments on his exegesis of 1 Cor 14, where prophets are judged by the congregation due to their lower status. Gaffin and Farnell establish their arguments on Eph 2:20 where prophets are co-authoritative with the apostles. Analysis of OT leads to the same conclusions.

However, a more specialized study must be undertaken. Since the above arguments are concentrated on the function of the NT prophet, a study of prophetic content is better suited for an evaluation of accuracy. Agabus' prophecies provide a manageable sample. The question for this study concerns whether Agabus provides support for the fallible or the infallible view. Is Agabus a channel of prophecy that requires shifting between inferior elements and the divine elements, or are his prophecies completely accurate? The two prophecies of Agabus will be studied next.

# CHAPTER III

# FAMINE PROPHECY OF AGABUS

## Introduction

Agabus' first recorded prophecy occurs in Antioch.[118] A vibrant and diverse church is established in this city where Saul and Barnabas teach a large number of disciples who are the first to be called "Christians" (Acts 11:19-26).[119] A year later, a caravan of prophets arrive from

Jerusalem (Acts 11:27). The only name identified in this group is Agabus. Before an assembly of believers in Antioch, Agabus delivers his prophecy (Acts 11:28).[120] Rainer Riesner suggests that the prophecy was delivered during the last two years of Caligula in 40/41 AD, but no later than 44 AD when Herod Agrippa died.[121] Luke

---

[118] For the historical background of Antioch, see Merrill C. Tenney, "The Influence of Antioch on Apostolic Christianity," *BSac* 107 (1950) 299-302.

[119] For a discussion of the word "Christians" and its origins, see I. Howard Marshall, *The Acts of the Apostles: An Introduction and Commentary* (Tyndale New Testament Commentaries 5; Grand Rapids: Eerdmans, 1980) 203.

[120] The more vivid reading found in Codex Bezae is not needed to infer that the prophetic activity took place in an assembly. Regardless, most of the MSS do not support the reading. Joseph A. Fitzmyer, *The Acts of the Apostles: A New Translation with Introduction and Commentary* (Anchor Bible 31; New York: Doubleday, 1998) 98.

[121] Rainer Riesner, *Paul's Early Period: Chronology, Mission Strategy, Theology* (trans. Doug Scott; Grand Rapids: Eerdmans, 1998) 134-35. If one assumes that Luke wrote his account in a chronological order, the connection between Acts 11 and 12 is especially helpful in dating the prophecy. The delivery of the prophecy (Acts 11:28) takes

presents the prophecy in a summary format, narrating the following: ἀναστὰς δὲ εἷς ἐξ αὐτῶν ὀνόματι Ἄγαβος ἐσήμανεν διὰ τοῦ πνεύματος λιμὸν μεγάλην μέλλειν ἔσεσθαι ἐφ' ὅλην τὴν οἰκουμένην (Agabus stood and signified through the Spirit that a great famine was about to take place over the whole world) (Acts 11:28).[122] Since future events are foretold, the prophecy is a prediction.

In retrospect, Luke finds Agabus credible. The author adds that this event took place during the reign of Claudius (ἥτις ἐγένετο ἐπὶ Κλαυδίου) (Acts 11:28). According to Bruce, Claudius ruled as the fourth Roman emperor from 41 AD until 54 AD.[123] If one accepts Luke's testimony, the prophecy must be fulfilled within those dates. So then, the prophecy was fulfilled some time during 41-54 AD.

A question remains however, concerning the accuracy of the prophecy: Is Agabus' prophecy accurate in its details? Such a study requires a careful observation of Luke's vocabulary and numerous sources that describe the famine. It is helpful then, to first analyze the various words and phrases employed by Luke to describe Agabus' prophecy. It is also helpful to study whether the details of Roman history amount to a λιμὸν μεγάλην... ἐφ' ὅλην τὴν οἰκουμένην (great famine...upon the whole world). Thence, it will be seen whether Agabus is indeed fallible or infallible in details.

---

place before the death of Herod Agrippa, described in Acts 12. Thus, 44 AD is the appropriate *terminus ad quem*. See also C. K. Barret, *A Critical and Exegetical Commentary on the Acts of the Apostles* (ICC; 2 Vols; Edinburgh: T&T Clark, 1994) 1:563-64.

[122] All translations from the Bible are from the present writer, unless indicated otherwise. For general background information on famines, see Craig S. Keener, *Acts: An Exegetical Commentary: Volume 2: 3:1-14:28* (Grand Rapids: Baker Academic, 2013) 1853-55.

[123] F. F. Bruce, *The Acts of the Apostles: Greek Text with Introduction and Commentary* (Grand Rapids: Eerdmans, 1990) 276.

## Nature of the Famine Prophecy

The three disputed issues concerning the famine prophecy concern its speech, its source, and its scope. These three issues can be resolved somewhat through a lexical/word study of three following words/phrases, respectively: 1) ἐσήμανεν (signified); 2) διὰ τοῦ πνεύματος (through the Spirit); and 3) ἐφ' ὅλην τὴν οἰκουμένην (upon the whole world). A proper understanding of these words is foundational to a correct assessment of prophetic accuracy.

*The speech of the prophecy: analysis of "signify"*

The first disputed word of Acts 11:28 is ἐσήμανεν (signified). The word means either 1) "to make known, *report, communicate*; 2) to intimate something respecting the future, *indicate, suggest, intimate*; or 3) to provide an explanation for something that is enigmatic, *mean, signify.*"[124] In order to understand the prophecy, one must determine the manner in which Agabus spoke it. Though one can be vague without being inaccurate, Grudem opines that the verb in question suggests imprecision. He writes:

> A degree of imprecision is also suggested by the word translated "foretold" (Greek *sēmainō*, "signified, indicated"). This same word was used in extra-biblical literature (such as the Jewish writer Josephus or the secular writer Plutarch) of prophetic speech "that simply gives a vague indication of what is to happen," and we may conclude that absolute divine authority is neither required nor ruled out by this description.[125]

---

[124]BDAG, 920.

[125]Grudem, *The Gift of Prophecy in the New Testament and Today*, 2

Alternately, there are scholars who hold that "signify" is a clear method of communication. Ernst Haenchen concludes that the verb is "not allusive or symbolic but prophecy."[126] Hans Conzelmann indicates that the word implies "clear announcements," even though some secular sources do not employ the word in such a manner.[127] A word study of the verb can help in determining the exact nuance of the word.

*"Signify" in biblical literature*

The word is found 26 times in the Greek OT (Septuagint or LXX), six times in NT, and in several Greco-Roman sources. The usage of the word in each type of literature aids in better understanding the word in the context of Acts 11:28.

In the LXX and the NT, the word is most often used to describe communication of clear, detailed information. This usage is found 17 out of 26 times.[128] So, more than half the time the verb is used to convey lucid information. The following examples are illustrative: 1) teaching of the correct ways of God (Exo 18:20); 2) instruction to build the temple in Jerusalem (1 Esdras 2:2); 3) a list of names revealed (1 Esdras 8:48); 4) an exposure of an assassination plot (Est 2:22); 5) a subject mentioned in context by a writer (2 Macc 2:1; c.f. 2 Macc

---

[126]Ernst Haenchen, *The Acts of the Apostles: A Commentary* (trans. by Bernard Noble and Gerald Shinn; Oxford: Blackwell, 1987) 374.

[127]Hans Conzelmann, *The Acts of the Apostles* (Hermeneia; Philadelphia: Fortress, 1987) 90.

[128]Word studies yield the following definition groups: 1) communication of clear, detailed information, 17 times (Exo 18:20; 1 Esdras 2:2; 8:48; Esth 2:22; 3:13; 2 Macc 2:1; 11:17; Ezek 33:3; Dan 2:15, 23, 30, 45; John 12:33; 18:32; 21:18; Acts 25:27; Rev 1:1); 2) tonic, encrypted communicative sounds, such as horns or whistles, 10 times (Num 10:9; Josh 6:8; 2 Chr 13:12; Neh 8:15; Job 39:24, 25; Zech 10:8; Jer 4:5; 6:1; Ezek 33:6); 3) shouting, three times (Judges 7:21 (2); Ezra 3:11); and 4) gestures, once (Prov 6:13).

1:19-33); 6) a warning of an approaching enemy (Ezek 33:3); 7) an initiation of a royal decree (Dan 2:15); and 8) a prophetic dream and its interpretation (Dan 2:23, 30, 45). One cannot expect to convey such information vaguely and achieve the desired results. OT testimony weighs against Grudem's definition of "signify."

NT evidence also solidifies the normal usage of this verb. Three times the word is used to describe death sentences. First, when Jesus says: κἀγὼ ἐὰν ὑψωθῶ ἐκ τῆς γῆς, πάντας ἑλκύσω πρὸς ἐμαυτόν (And if I am lifted up from the earth I will draw all to myself), John narrates that He "signified" the kind of death He would die (John 12:32-33). The significant information gathered in this prophecy is that Jesus would die in abeyance, so that certain forms of death such as stoning or drowning would be ruled out. Secondly, when the Jews tell Pilate that they could not execute Jesus, John again narrates that the word that Christ "signified" earlier is about to be fulfilled (John 18:32-33). Since crucifixion is a Roman form of punishment, not Jewish, this verse provides another clue concerning the form of death Jesus faces later.

Lastly, Jesus predicts the death of Peter in the following manner: ἀμὴν ἀμὴν λέγω σοι, ὅτε ἦς νεώτερος, ἐζώννυες σεαυτὸν καὶ περιεπάτεις ὅπου ἤθελες· ὅταν δὲ γηράσῃς, ἐκτενεῖς τὰς χεῖράς σου, καὶ ἄλλος σε ζώσει καὶ οἴσει ὅπου οὐ θέλεις (Truly, truly I say to you, when you were younger, you girded yourself and walked where you wanted; but when you grow old, you will extend your hands, and another will gird you and will carry you where you do not want to go) (John 21:18). John narrates in the following verse that Jesus just "signified" another prediction of death, albeit this time the subject is Peter (John 21:19). Such indication is not vague, but rather vivid. Also, if Peter speaks of this event in 2 Peter 1:14, it is notable that Peter says, ὁ κύριος ἡμῶν Ἰησοῦς Χριστὸς ἐδήλωσέν μοι (our Lord Jesus

Christ made it clear to me). Jesus predicts rather vividly and precisely that Peter will face a forced death, not a natural one.

John certainly used "signify" to communicate precise and clear prophecy. Though all of the details are not provided, John surmises from the words of Jesus, Pilate, and the Jews the kind of death which Peter and Jesus Himself would die. The latter would suffer death whereby He is lifted up from the earth, while the former would suffer death at a later age when another person will clothe and carry him. Rev 1:1 also indicates that the entire Apocalypse is a "signified" product of revelation from God and Christ. John the Apostle employs this word to describe the relay of prophetic communication.

The rest of NT does not support the idea of imprecision. In Acts 25:24-27, Festus entreats an investigation of Paul from King Agrippa because he does not have anything definite to write to his superior (περὶ οὗ ἀσφαλές τι γράψαι τῷ κυρίῳ οὐκ ἔχω) (Acts 25:26). Without any significant details, it is absurd for Festus to send a prisoner without "signifying" the charges against him (ἄλογον γάρ μοι δοκεῖ πέμποντα δέσμιον μὴ καὶ τὰς κατ' αὐτοῦ αἰτίας σημᾶναι). If Grudem's definition is correct, and Festus truly desires to communicate the details behind the reason for Paul's arrest, it would not make sense for the Roman official to use the word "signify."

### "Signify" in secular literature

Thus far, neither the LXX nor the NT lend major support to Grudem's idea of vagueness in "signify." Secular sources such as Josephus do not support such an idea either. In fact, the word is used to introduce or summarize inspired prophetic speech in various OT accounts.[129]

---

[129]The following are the prophetic statements that are "signified"

Yet there are secular literatures where "signify" is describing cultic and perhaps vague prophecy. Plutarch writes: "I imagine that you are familiar with the saying found in Heracleitus to the effect that the Lord whose prophetic shrine is at Delphi neither tells nor conceals, but indicates."[130] Plutarch's saying certainly allows for vagueness in the word "signify," since the meaning of the word is embedded somewhere between plain and concealed speech.

The word is found again in the context of superstition, portent, and augury. Before heading into his final battle, a Spartan admiral named Callicratidas is described by Plutarch:

> "As he offered sacrifice before the battle, and heard from the seer that the indications of the omens were victory for the army, but death for its commander, he said, not at all disconcerted, 'Sparta's fate rests not with one man...'"[131]

Concerning an earthquake during tense times of war, Thucydides writes: "This was said and believed to be ominous of coming events, and indeed every other incident of the sort which chanced to occur was carefully looked into."[132]

---

in the history of Israel: 1) the prophecy of Samuel concerning the identify of the first king of Israel; 2) the prophecy of Nathan concerning the uprising of David's son; 3) the prophecy of Zedekiah concerning victory over Syria; and 4) the prophecy of Daniel concerning the death of Belshazzar and the overthrow of Babylon. Josephus, *Jewish Antiquities* 6:50 § 190-91; 7:214 § 474-75; 8:409 § 792-93; 10:241 § 290-91.

[130]Plutarch, *Moralia* 404 E § 314-15.

[131]Ibid., 222 F § 333-34.

[132]Thucydides, *The History of the Peloponnesian War* 2:8:3 § 272-73.

Another important source by Epictetus is also enlightening. While arguing that "the interpreter" should not be overly exalted in gaining understanding, he uses cultic examples to support his thesis. The following quote clearly demonstrates the cultic nuance of "signify":

> No more have we need of him who divines through sacrifice, considered on his own account, but simply because we think that through his instrumentality we shall understand the future and the signs given by the gods; nor do we need the entrails on their own account, but only because through them the signs are given; nor do we admire the crow or the raven, but God, who gives His signs through them. Wherefore, I go to this interpreter and diviner and say, "Examine for me the entrails, and tell me what signs they give."[133]

*"Signify" in Acts 11:28.*

One can generally conclude from the LXX, NT, and Greco-Roman sources that the verb "signify" is a word that can be used to describe prophetic phenomena. While some secular sources hint vagueness in the meaning of this word, the writers of the Bible, as well as Josephus, use this word to describe prophecy that they deem to be clear. Since Luke is a biblical writer in his own right, and since he considers this prophecy to be fulfilled, it is likely that "signify" here describes lucid, inspired prophecy (Acts 11:28).

*The source of the prophecy: analysis of "through the Spirit"*

In order to understand the sort of speech that is dealt with in Acts 11:28, the phrase διὰ τοῦ πνεύματος (through the Spirit) must be analyzed.

---

[133] Epictetus, *Arrian's Discourses of Epictetus* 1:17:18 § 118-19.

Grudem believes there is room for error based on amalgamation of human influence with divine revelation. He writes:

> When Luke says that Agabus foretold "by the Spirit" he uses a phrase (Greek *dia tou pneumatou*) which is never used in the Greek Old Testament (the Septuagint) to refer to prophetic speech. The word *dia* ("through" or "by means of") seems to signify "the originator of an action," and this construction would be well suited to express a rather loose relationship between the Holy Spirit and the prophet, since it allows room for a large degree of personal influence by the human person himself.[134]

Grudem reaches this conclusion based on an entry of a standard lexicon.[135] Indeed, Grudem may be correct that the attention of this prepositional phrase (διὰ τοῦ πνεύματος) is on the "originator" of the prophetic activity: the Holy Spirit.[136] The prepositional phrase shows "a marker of personal agency...with focus on the originator of an action."[137] Grudem allows for mistakes in the transmission of revelation since the agent is human.

However, one wonders whether Grudem can justly legitimize his view from this phrase that there is a loose relationship between the Holy Spirit and Agabus. There are three reasons for doubts. First, the syntax simply cannot determine whether the relationship between the agent and the originator is loose or tight. The emphasis

---

[134] Grudem, *The Gift of Prophecy in the New Testament and Today*, 71-72.

[135] BAGD, 180, III. 2. b.

[136] Grudem, *The Gift of Prophecy in the New Testament and Today*, 71-72. See also BDAG, 225, 4. b.

[137] BDAG, 225, 4. b.

on the "originator" does not exclude a tight relationship between the Holy Spirit and Agabus.

Secondly, if one has reasons to distrust Agabus as a faithful transmitter based on this prepositon-articlegenitive noun construction, other figures such as the apostle Paul must also be doubted. In 1 Thessalonians 4:2, Paul writes: οἴδατε γὰρ τίνας παραγγελίας ἐδώκαμεν ὑμῖν διὰ τοῦ κυρίου Ἰησοῦ (For you know what commands we gave to you through Lord Jesus). Is one to doubt whether the Apostle Paul has a close relationship with Christ? Is there allowance for a "large degree of personal influence" from Paul based on the prepositional construction? [138] Syntax simply cannot answer such questions.

The third reason to doubt Grudem's conclusion is that other scholars have not shared Grudem's syntactical conclusions. For example, Nigel Turner observes that Acts 11:28 provides an example of Christian prophecy and Agabus spoke directly from God.[139] Max Turner, who would otherwise support Grudem, does not share a hint of his conclusion concerning "through the Spirit" and other similar phrases:

> In all instances of this group the language is probably to be taken literally, and the sense is usually the immediately apparent one. For example, when Luke says that men spoke 'through' (*dia*) the Holy Spirit, he means they spoke charismatically; i.e. that God, by the

---

[138] A. T. Robertson writes in his grammar that the matter seems turned around in 1 Thessalonians 4:2, but even as Paul was the speaker, he conceives Christ as the One who commands. The context, not the syntax, must determine the relationship between the agent and the originator. A. T. Robertson, *A Grammar of the Greek New Testament in the Light of Historical Research* (Nashville: Broadman, 1934) 583.

[139] Nigel Turner, *Grammatical Insights into the New Testament* (Edinburgh: T. & T. Clark, 1965) 21.

Spirit, prompted the wording and/or empowered the utterance of the message in question.[140]

Thus, the discussion concerning the preposition, article, and noun in Acts 11:28 is another exegetical hotbed for the fallible/infallible prophecy debate. The study of this important phrase leads to the LXX and NT where the contexts surrounding the various occurrences can be observed. One can analyze various passages that contain "through" and "Spirit" to observe whether Grudem is correct to the effect that the speaker and the Spirit indeed have a loose relationship (Exo 15:8; Isa 30:1; Odes 1:8; Acts 1:2; 4:25; 21:4; Rom 5:5; 1 Cor 2:10; 12:8; Eph 3:16; 2 Thess 2:2; 2 Tim 1:14; Heb 9:14). Lukan usages of this phrase will be studied last.

### "Through the Spirit" outside Acts

The phrase in discussion is found ten times outside of Acts. In the LXX, "through the Spirit" is found in Exodus 15:1, Isaiah 30:1, and Odes 1:8. According to the accounts of Moses concerning the Red Sea, "the waters parted through the breath of His anger" (Exo 15:1; Odes 1:8). In Isaiah 30:1, Israelites could have made political plans that originate from God, but they fail to do so. Isaiah records: "Woe to the rebellious children, thus says the Lord. You made a plan, not through me, and a treaty, not through my Spirit, to add sin upon sin." There is nothing to suggest that there is a loose relationship between God and His breath, and between God and His treaty in the LXX.

In the NT, the phrase is found in seven verses. In Romans 5:5, the apostle Paul writes that ἡ ἀγάπη τοῦ θεοῦ ἐκκέχυται ἐν ταῖς καρδίαις ἡμῶν διὰ πνεύματος ἁγίου τοῦ δοθέντος ἡμῖν (the love of God has been

---

[140]Max Turner, "Spirit Endowment In Luke/Acts: Some Linguistic Considerations," *Vox Evangelica* 12 (1981) 45.

poured out in our hearts through the Holy Spirit who was given to us). In another epistle, Paul teaches how ἀπεκάλυψεν ὁ θεὸς διὰ τοῦ πνεύματος (God has revealed through the Spirit) all that He had prepared for those who love Him (1 Cor 2:9-10). In the same epistle, Paul explains that ᾧ μὲν γὰρ διὰ τοῦ πνεύματος δίδοται λόγος σοφίας (for on one hand, to one is given word of wisdom through the Spirit) (1 Cor 12:8). In Ephesians 3:16, Paul prays that God would grant the Ephesian church δυνάμει κραταιωθῆναι διὰ τοῦ πνεύματος αὐτοῦ εἰς τὸν ἔσω ἄνθρωπον (to be strengthened with power through His Spirit in the inner man). These four verses from Paul's epistles do not imply a loose relationship between God and the Holy Spirit.

In 2 Thessalonians 2:2, Paul asks for calmness among the Thessalonian believers and that they resist any false teachings concerning the second advent of Christ. Paul clarifies that such disturbances should be avoided whether they are sourced μήτε διὰ πνεύματος μήτε διὰ λόγου μήτε δι' ἐπιστολῆς ὡς δι' ἡμῶν (through a spirit, a word, or a letter as if through us). A false teaching may come through a false spirit. In 2 Timothy 1:14, Paul charges Timothy to τὴν καλὴν παραθήκην φύλαξον διὰ πνεύματος ἁγίου τοῦ ἐνοικοῦντος ἐν ἡμῖν (guard the good deposit through the Holy Spirit that dwells in you). There is no hint of a loose relationship between Timothy and the indwelling Spirit.

Lastly, the writer of Hebrews writes concerning Christ, ὃς διὰ πνεύματος αἰωνίου ἑαυτὸν προσήνεγκεν ἄμωμον τῷ θεῷ (who through the eternal Spirit offered Himself unblemished to God) (Heb 9:14). Jesus' sacrifice is made through the Spirit. There is no reason to question the relationship between the Son and the Spirit.

Thus far, there is no validity in evaluating the relationship between the agent and the originator when the prepositional phrase, "through the Spirit" is found.

There are two reasons for this conclusion. First, Moses, Isaiah, Paul, and the writer of Hebrews employ the phrase without regard for quality of relationships between the originator and the agent. Also, to be completely objective, if Grudem is correct concerning the prepositional phrase, all of the above verses must be reexamined and the relationships between the persons of the Trinity must be doubted.

### *"Through the Spirit" in Acts*

In Acts there are three passages besides Acts 11:28 where the prepositional phrase in discussion is found. In Acts 1:2, Jesus was taken up in ascension after ἐντειλάμενος τοῖς ἀποστόλοις διὰ πνεύματος ἁγίου οὓς ἐξελέξατο ἀνελήμφθη (commanding the apostles through the Holy Spirit). In Acts 4:25, God is ὁ τοῦ πατρὸς ἡμῶν διὰ πνεύματος ἁγίου στόματος Δαυὶδ παιδός σου εἰπών (the One who spoke from our father through the Holy Spirit from the mouth of David your servant). In these two verses, there are interactions between the persons of the Trinity. The end result is an inspired psalm without any suggestion that the revelation of God is diminished because of David, the prophetic agent.

Acts 21:4 is a much-disputed passage. In this verse, Paul arrives in Tyre, where he meets disciples οἵτινες τῷ Παύλῳ ἔλεγον διὰ τοῦ πνεύματος μὴ ἐπιβαίνειν εἰς Ἱεροσόλυμα (who were telling Paul through the Spirit to not embark into Jerusalem). However, Paul proceeds to Jerusalem anyway and it appears that the prophetic message is deliberately disregarded, perhaps due to its inferior quality. Grudem writes:

> This verse does not mention prophecy directly, but the parallel with Acts 11:28, where human speech activity "through the Spirit" is explicitly attributed to the prophet Agabus, suggests that these disciples were in fact prophesying. (In contrast to Acts 13:2, human

spokesmen are here explicitly credited with the warning.) But if this really is a report of prophesying, as it certainly seems to be, then it is very significant for understanding the nature of prophetic authority in ordinary New Testament congregations. It is significant because Paul simply disobeyed their words, something he would not have done if he had thought that they were speaking the very words of God.[141]

Consequently, in Grudem's mind, this "coupling" of prophetic report and false interpretation is the result of the "loose relationship" between the prophet and the Spirit. This sort of relationship is implied from the prepositional phrase. Witherington sides with Grudem and concludes that what results from this mixture is a need for the sifting process prescribed in 1 Cor 14.[142] So then, as Jervell observes, while Paul is subservient to the Spirit-inspired Scriptures, the apostle willingly disobeys the Spirit-inspired NT prophets.[143]

There are some issues with this interpretation of Acts 21:4. Grudem and those with him assume that the disciples of Tyre must be speaking prophecy because they speak "through the Spirit." But is that really the case? Just because there is congregational speaking through the

---

[141]Grudem, *The Gift of Prophecy in the New Testament and Today*, 75.

[142]Ben Witherington III, *The Acts of the Apostles: A Socio-Rhetorical Commentary* (Grand Rapids: Eerdmans/Carlisle, UK: Paternoster, 1998) 630-31.

[143]J. Jervell, *The Theology of the Acts of the Apostles* (New Testament Theology; Cambridge: Cambridge University Press, 1996) 51. Gentry offers the possibility that Paul is in error here and sins (Acts 15:38-39; Rom 7). However, Harrison rejects such serious charges because Paul has a history of submission to revelation (Acts 20:23; 22:17-21; Gal 2:2). Gentry, Jr., *The Charismatic Gift of Prophecy*, 38-39; E. F. Harrison, *Acts: The Expanding Church* (Chicago: Moody, 1975) 322.

Spirit that does not mean all speaking is prophecy. Tongues, interpretation, wisdom, knowledge, exhortation and teaching also take place in the body and originate from the Spirit (Rom 12:3-8; 1 Cor 12:4-11). But Paul has no qualms about subjugating the Spirit-given gift of tongues-speech under the authority of the Spirit-given prophecy-speech (1 Cor 14). Also, as discussed above, Isaiah 30:1 implies that there is a proper way to plan "through the Spirit." Does that mean that planning should be equated with prophecy just because both are done through the Spirit? Is godly planning infallible and inerrant? Similarly, gifted disciples of Tyre could be offering their spirit-motivated exhortation, not new prophecy.

Thus, it is better to sharply draw the line between prophetic revelation and non-prophetic application.[144] The prepositional phrase does not imply that prophets amalgamate their ideas with divine messages.[145] Instead of mixing revelation and interpretation, they are kept completely separate, though given in one setting.[146] Based on one divine revelation, two different human responses are observed. The predictions of Paul's sufferings are

---

[144] Craig S. Keener, *Acts: An Exegetical Commentary: Volume 3:15:1-23:35* (Grand Rapids: Baker Academic, 2014)

[145] Longenecker suggests an alternative option for understanding the prepositional phrase: "Their trying to dissuade him 'through the Spirit' (*dia tou pneumatos*) from going on to Jerusalem may mean that the Spirit was ordering Paul not to continue with his plans. In that case his determination to proceed was disobedience to the Spirit. Or it may be that Paul doubted the inspiration of these Tyrian believers. Probably, however, we should understand the preposition *dia* ('through') as meaning that the Spirit's message was the occasion for the believer's concern rather than that their trying to dissuade Paul was directly inspired by the Spirit. So, in line with 19:21 and 20:22-24, we should treat this not as Paul's rejection of a prophetic oracle but as another case of the Spirit's revelation to Christian prophets of what lay in store for Paul at Jerusalem and of his new friends' natural desire to dissuade him (cf. vv. 10-15)." Longenecker, "The Acts of the Apostles," 9:516.

[146] Gaffin Jr., "A Cessationist View," 49-50.

understood by his friends as warnings to turn back, while Paul himself applies the warnings as preparatory measures.[147] The protective instincts of the Tyrian disciples are set against the inclination of the Spirit revealed earlier (Acts 20:22-23). Regardless, that which is called "prophecy" ends with the warning and does not extend to the application of the congregation, which includes the prophet.[148]

However, all of these conclusions are premature, whether the ideas are from Grudem or his opponents. One cannot assess NT prophecy fairly without any explicit prophetic content, found wanting in Acts 21:4.[149] The *crux interpretum* is Acts 21:11, where Agabus' words are recorded.[150] Basing any conclusions on a prepositional

---

[147]Barret, *A Critical and Exegetical Commentary on the Acts of the Apostles*, 2:990. Conzelmann, *The Acts of the Apostles*, 178; Harrison, *Acts*, 320, 322; John Calvin, *The Acts of the Apostles: Chapters 14-28* (trans. John W. Fraser; ed. David W. Torrance and Thomas F. Torrance; Grand Rapids: Eerdmans, 1966) 193. D. J. Williams, *Acts* (New International Biblical Commentary 5; Peabody, MA: Hendrickson, 1990) 360; Simon J. Kistemaker, *Acts* (New Testament Commentary; Grand Rapids: Baker, 1990) 745-46; Aijith Fernando, *Acts* (NIV Application Commentary; Grand Rapids: Zondervan, 1998) 558-59; Richard N. Longenecker, "The Acts of the Apostles," *Expositor's Bible Commentary* (ed. F. Gaebelein; 12 vols; Grand Rapids: Zondervan, 1981) 9:516; William M. Ramsay, *St. Paul: The Traveler and Roman Citizen* (revised and updated by Mark Wilson; Grand Rapids: Kregel, 2001) 228.

[148]To Grudem and Storms however, "prophecy" not only includes the received revelation, but the response as well. This definition is where Grudem's differs from Gaffin. He writes: "There is a revelation from the Holy Spirit to the disciples at Tyre, and in response to that revelation they tell Paul not to go to Jerusalem. The difference in our viewpoints is that I would call the response or report of that revelation a 'prophecy,' and Gaffin would not." Grudem, *The Gift of Prophecy in the New Testament and Today*, 76; Storms, *Practicing the Power*, 114.

[149]The biblical language often features "vagueness of economy," so that every minute detail is not recorded. See George B. Caird, *The Language and Imagery of the Bible* (Philadelphia: Westminster, 1980) 93-94.

[150]These verses will be studied in the next chapter.

phrase alone is unwarranted. Grudem's point on Acts 11:28 and Acts 21:4 is moot.

Thus, in conclusion, the source of Agabus' prophecy in Acts 11:28 is undoubtedly the Holy Spirit. There are several reasons to assume this view. First, one simply cannot make any bold statements concerning NT prophecy based on a prepositional phrase. Secondly, the contextual passages that contain the phrase διὰ τοῦ πνεύματος (through the Spirit) do not strongly suggest a loose relationship between the human and the Holy Spirit. Nine out of thirteen verses discussed above describe relationships between the persons in the Trinity. Thirdly, Acts 21:4 is only an adumbration of trouble ahead for Paul and reveal no prophetic content. Whether NT prophets mix their opinions with divine messages can only be determined if the actual words are available, as in Acts 21:11.[151] Thus in Acts 11:28, the source of Agabus' prophecy is the Holy Spirit.

*The scope of the prophecy: analysis of "the whole world"*

Though not as controversial as the previously studied phrases, ἐφ' ὅλην τὴν οἰκουμένην (upon the whole world) must be properly defined to observe what amounts to an accurate fulfillment. According to BDAG, the word can be defined as either 1) "the earth as inhabited area, exclusive of the heavens above and nether regions, the inhabited earth, the world," 2) "the world as administrative unit, the Roman Empire," 3) "all inhabitants of the earth," or 4) an extraordinary, supernatural world.[152]

---

[151]As Marguerat suggests, the deliberate ambiguity that leads to narrative tensions may be a feature of Luke's literary design, used to stimulate the reader. The anxious reader must continue in the narrative to discover the fate of Paul. Marguerat, *The First Christian Historian*, 51-52.

[152]BDAG, 699-700. See also LSJ, 1205.

Some have defined this phrase literally, while others have understood the phrase in a hyperbolic manner. If the famine is predicted to come upon the entire geographical world, then Agabus' prophecy is fulfilled only partially. On the other hand, if the famine is restricted to the political world of Rome or the region of Judea, the possibility of an accurate, complete fulfillment is debatable. All three possibilities will be explored.

*Word study of "the whole world"*

The word "world" (οἰκουμένη) occurs 65 times in the LXX and the NT. "Whole" (ὅλος) and "world" (οἰκουμένη) are combined in sixteen instances.[153] In a similar phrase, "all" (πᾶς) and "world" (οἰκουμένη) are combined thrice in Est 3:13, Dan 2:38, and Luke 2:1.

The word οἰκουμένη describes the entire globe most of the time.[154] Often times in Psalms, God executes His ways in the entire globe. Other times, because a nation or a ruler has influence that is so great, his or its acts and reign could be seen as worldwide (1 Esdras 2:2; Est 3:13 (2); Dan 2:38). Lastly, there is a legitimate reason to take this word as a political term, as in "empire," referring to an entire nation (Dan 3:2 (2); Luke 2:1).

---

[153] 2 Macc 2:22; Odes 7:45; Isa 10:14, 23; 13:5, 9, 11; 14:17, 26; 37:18; Epistle of Jeremiah 1:61; Dan 3:45; Matt 24:14; Rev 3:10; 12:9; 16:14.

[154] Word studies yield the following results: 1) literal usage, 45 times (2 Sam 22:16; Ps 9:8; 18:15; 19:4; 24:1; 33:8; 49:1; 50:12; 72:8; 77:18; 89:11; 90:2; 93:1; 96:10, 13; 97:4; 98:7, 9; Odes 7:45; Prov 8:31; Wis 1:7; Isa 10:14; 13:11;14:26 (2); 24:1, 4; 27:6; 34:1; 37:16; Jer 10:12; 51:15; Epistle of Jeremiah 1:61; Dan 3:45; Dan TH 3:45; Matt 24:14; Luke 4:5; 21:26; Acts 17:31; Rom 10:18; Heb 1:6; 2:5; Rev 3:10;12:9; 16:14); 2) figurative, hyperbolic, eleven times (1 Esdras 2:2; Esth 3:13 (2); 2 Macc 2:22; Isa 23:17; 37:18; Lam 4:12; Dan 2:38; Acts 17:6; 19:27; 24:5); 3) political area, eight times (Isa 10:23; 13:5, 9; 14:17; 62:4; Dan 3:2 (2); Luke 2:1).

*The meaning of "the whole world"*

So, then, what is the scope of Agabus prophecy? Charles C. Torrey believes Luke means to describe the Palestine region. In this view, Luke is envisioned as a translator of an original Aramaic source of Acts 1-15 who misunderstands and exaggerates the phrase "all the land."[155] However, such an amateur mistake is unlikely, and in fact, unfit for any translator of Aramaic, according to De Zwaan and others.[156]

A more plausible alternative, substantiated by statistics gathered above, is offered by Martin Hengel. The predictions of Agabus may have been further details concerning world-wide famine conditions of the end times (Mark 13:8).[157] With this view, the literal meaning of ἐφ' ὅλην τὴν οἰκουμένην (upon the whole world) is preserved.

However, there are some glaring weaknesses with this view. In the very verse which presents Agabus' prophecy, Luke records that the prophecy was fulfilled during the reign of Claudius (Acts 11:28). Indeed, the Roman Empire may have dealt with much turmoil during Claudius' reign, but the world-at-large does not record famines at that time. The scope of Mark 13:8 is wider and the famine conditions described therein could not have been missed before the eyes of the world. A more manageable famine would have been verifiable by Luke. If Luke is inspired by the Spirit to record Scripture, he can

---

[155] Charles C. Torrey, *The Composition and the Date of Acts* (Cambridge: Harvard University Press, 1916) 20-21.

[156] J. De Zwaan, "The Use of the Greek Language in Acts," *Beginnings of Christianity: Part I: The Acts of the Apostles* (ed. F. J. Foakes Jackson and Kirsopp Lake; 5 vols; Grand Rapids: Baker, 1979) 2:59; Bruce, *The Acts of the Apostles*, 276; Haenchen, *The Acts of the Apostles*, 374; J. H. Moulton, and N. Turner, *A Grammar of New Testament Greek* (4 vols; Edinburgh: T&T Clark, 1976) 2:474.

[157] Martin Hengel, *Acts and the History of the Earliest Christianity* (Philadelphia: Fortress Press 1979) 111.

be trusted for an accurate summary and an honest assessment of the prophecy.

So then, the best way of understanding ἐφ' ὅλην τὴν οἰκουμένην (upon the whole world) is to define the phrase in context as the entire Roman empire.[158] This appears to be the commonly accepted view.[159] One support comes from Luke's familiarity with the political understanding of "world" (οἰκουμένη). In a similar phrase, Luke combines "all" (πᾶς) and "world" (οἰκουμένη) to describe an empire-wide census (Luke 2:1).[160] Interestingly enough, Luke names Augustus, another Caesar, alongside the phrase in Luke 2:1. The names of Caesars have a restrictive effect on the phrase "all the world."[161]

---

[158] The New International Version of the Bible interprets the phrase correctly: "over the entire Roman world"

[159] See Fitzmeyer, *The Acts of the Apostles*, 481; Marshall, *The Acts of the Apostles*, 203-04; Harrison, *Acts*, 186; Williams, *Acts*, 206; Kistemaker, *Acts*, 425; R. B. Rackham, *The Acts of the Apostles: An Exposition* (Westminster Commentaries; London: Methuen, 1901) 173; William J. Larkin Jr., *Acts* (IVP New Testament Commentary 5; Downer's Grove, IL: InterVarsity, 1995) 179-80; Luke Timothy Johnson, *The Acts of the Apostles* (Sacra Pagina 5; Collegeville, MN: The Liturgical Press, 1991) 205-06; B. R. Gaventa, *Acts* (Abingdon New Testament Commentaries; Nashville: Abingdon, 2003) 181.

[160] Also, Luke uses "world" (oivkoume,nh) in several different senses elsewhere (Luke 4:5; Acts 17:6; 24:5). However, the intended meaning in those verses is not necessarily "political" as Johnson asserts. The best clue for the political meaning is the naming of Roman Emperors. Johnson, *The Acts of the Apostles*, 205-06.

[161] Secular sources also qualify "world" with names of political leaders in context for the desired effect of describing the Roman Empire. Of particular interest are Josephus and Lucian. The former writes concerning the "world" under Rome with various political leaders on the move: "And now Vespasian took along with him his army from Antioch, (which is the metropolis of Syria, and, without dispute, deserves the place of the third city in the habitable earth that was under the Roman empire, {a} both in size and other marks of prosperity,) where he found King Agrippa, with all his forces, waiting for his coming, and marched to Ptolemais." Josephus, *The Jewish Wars* 3.29 § 582-85. The next example from Lucian is especially important,

*Summary*

The analyses of Agabus' prophecy produce the following understanding of the prophetic message: 1) The prophecy is cogent, predictive speech; 2) The prophecy is sourced in the Holy Spirit without human influence; 3) The prophecy pertains to the entire Roman world. With a clear understanding of the famine prophecy one can proceed to verify its contents. The contents can be verified both from the Scriptures and the historical events.

## Fulfillment of the Prophecy

Having analyzed the important words and phrases of Acts 11:28, the famine prophecy can be evaluated with regard to its accuracy. The two main sources describing the famines during Claudius' reign are from Luke himself and from various secular sources.[162] All of the relevant sources will be scrutinized in detail.

---

since an emperor is mentioned in context, just as Luke mentions Claudius in Acts 11:28 and Augustus in Luke 2:1. Lucian writes: "I shall base the principal division of my treatise on their pursuits, and shall first tell you of the kings and the generals, one of whom the gracious dispensation of a great and godlike emperor has brought to the highest rank, thereby conferring a mighty boon upon the emperor's world." Unfortunately, the identity of the emperor is unknown. Possibilities include Antoninus Pius, Caracalla, and a host of others. Lucian, *The Octogenarians* 7 § 226-27.

[162]There is a possible supplemental source of information in the Scriptures concerning the fulfillment of Agabus' prophecy. In Gal 2:1-2, Paul recounts that he, with Barnabas and Titus went to Jerusalem in response to a "revelation." If this visit mentioned by Paul coincides with the visit recorded in Acts 11:30, Paul regarded Agabus' prophecy as an authoritative message from God that required a response. However, scholars are divided between two camps concerning Gal 2. For example, Fitzmeyer believes that Gal 2 is describing the events of Acts 15, not Acts 11. Witherington, on the other hand, is convinced through grammatical reasons to support the view that Gal 2 is describing Acts 11. If the visit of Gal 2:1-10 can be equated with the visit of Acts 11:30, one has in Gal 2:2 a verbal endorsement of Agabus' prophecy along with

*The fulfillment account of Luke*

Luke confirms that this prophecy was fulfilled during the reign of Claudius (Acts 11:28). Bock comments that Claudius was a nephew of Tiberius Caesar who ruled from AD 41 to 54 and administered well, but faced series of natural disasters during his reign.[163] If one assumes that Luke is an able historian, Agabus is confirmed as an accurate prophet.

Also, it is suspect to conclude that Agabus is wrong as a prophet here when he is welcomed without reservation in Acts 21:10-14. One must keep in mind that Acts 21:10-14 is a detailed account of prophetic revelation in a congregational setting. Where, then is the sifting process from the congregation in Caesarea, in order to bifurcate truth from error? Why are there no qualms concerning Agabus from Paul, Luke, and others in the narrative? Why does the congregation at Caesarea fear for Paul if Agabus' prophecies are not expected to come true in details? Luke records no judgment of Agabus' prophecy from the congregation of Caesarea.

*Secular sources concerning the famines*

Luke's confirmation of Agabus' prophecy is reason enough for confidence in its fulfillment, but extra-biblical sources lend additional support. Multiple famines during Claudius' reign are well-documented. There are, on one hand, sources that speak of general turmoil during the

---

Acts 21:10-14. However, since there is debate concerning the elements of this theory, no weighty arguments can be advanced. For discussion, see Fitzmeyer, *The Acts of the Apostles*, 480; Witherington III, *The Acts of the Apostles*, 375; David Wenham, "Acts and the Pauline Corpus II: The Evidence of Parallels," *The Book of Acts in Its Ancient Literary Setting* (ed. Bruce W. Winter and Andrew D. Clarke; The Book of Acts in Its First Century Setting 1; Grand Rapids: Eerdmans, 1993) 226-43. For a list of sources, see F. F. Bruce, *The Book of Acts* (NICNT; Grand Rapids: Eerdmans, 1988) 231.

[163]Darrell L. Bock, *Acts* (Baker Exegetical Commentary on the New Testament; Grand Rapids: Baker Academic, 2007) 417.

Caesar's reign. For example, Marshall explains that though no single disaster struck the whole world up to that point, there were frequent famines during the reign of Claudius according to Suetonius.[164] Bock cites an inscription from Asia Minor that describes a famine that seized the whole world.[165] Eusebius also confirms the fulfillment of the prophecy.[166]

On the other hand, there are individual famine accounts that affected several regions of the Roman Empire. Bruce cites Dio Cassius, the Michigan Papyri, Eusebius, and Tacitus for information on famines that struck Rome at the beginning of Claudius' reign, Egypt in the fifth year, Greece in the eighth or ninth year, and Rome again between the ninth and the eleventh years, respectively.[167] Closer to Antioch, Josephus relates how the famine struck Judea during the reign of Tiberius Alexander, from AD 46 to 48.[168]

The issue at hand concerns whether these famines accounts can be the secondary sources that further confirm Luke's confidence in Agabus. However, it is helpful to first observe the sources in detail.

*Local famines*

The first episode of the famines is recorded in the early part of the fifth century. Dio Cassius writes concerning Claudius' troubles with grain in Rome:

---

[164] Marshall, *The Acts of the Apostles*, 204.

[165] *CIG* (ed. A. Boeckh; 4 Vols; Berlin: Ex Officina Academica, 1828-77) 3973.5-6; Bock, *Acts*, 417-18.

[166] He writes: "In his time famine seized the world (and this also writers with a purpose quite other than ours have recorded in their histories), and so what the prophet Agabus had foretold, according to the Acts of the Apostles, that a famine would be over the whole world, received fulfillment." Eusebius, *Ecclesiastical History* 2.8.1 § 126-27.

[167] Keener, *Acts: An Exegetical Commentary: Volume 2: 3:1-14:28*, 1856-58; Bruce, *The Acts of the Apostles*, 276.

[168] Josephus, *Jewish Antiquities* 20.51-53 § 26-31.

> "On the occasion of a severe famine he considered the problem of providing an abundant food-supply, not only for that particular crisis but for all future time. For practically all the grain used by the Romans was imported, and yet the region near the mouth of the Tiber had no safe landing-places or suitable harbours, so that their mastery of the sea was rendered useless to them."[169]

As a result of this famine situation, Dio Cassius later records that Claudius took up an ambitious project to excavate huge portions of earth and build a harbor at about 42 AD.[170] Two facts can be gathered from the above source: 1) Claudius faced some difficult times at the beginning of his reign; and 2) Romans depended heavily on grain imports.

Other sources describe famine conditions elsewhere in the empire. For example, famines in Egypt are well-documented. Based on papyri from Tebtunis, an Egyptian city, Kenneth S. Gapp has gathered register documents which indicate that the grain prices averaged about eight drachmas per artaba in the late summer and the fall of 45 AD.[171] He notes that the grain prices in 3 AD, 33 AD, and 65 AD were less than half that amount.[172]

The main cause of the high prices is the unusually high Nile water level that took place during the reign of Claudius. Pliny the Elder observes:

---

[169]Dio Cassius, *Dio's Roman History* 60.11.1-2 § 392-93.

[170]Ibid., 60.11.3-5 § 394-95.

[171]Arthur E. R. Boak, Papyri *from Tebtunis, Part I* (Michigan Papyri, Vol. II; Ann Arbor: University of Michigan Press, 1933) 176, 194; Kenneth S. Gapp, "The Universal Famine under Claudius," *HTR* 28:4 (1935) 259.

[172]See footnote 7. Gapp, "The Universal Famine under Claudius," 259.

Its degrees of increase are detected by means of wells marked with a scale. An average rise is one of 24 feet. A smaller volume of water does not irrigate all localities, and a larger one by retiring too slowly retards agriculture; and the latter uses up the time for sowing because of the moisture of the soil, while the former gives no time for sowing because the soil is parched. The province takes careful note of both extremes: in a rise of 18 feet it senses famine, and even at 19.5 feet it begins to feel hungry, but 21 feet brings cheerfulness, 22.5 feet complete confidence and 24 feet delight. The largest rise up to date was one of 27 feet in the principate of Claudius, and the smallest 7.5 feet in the year of the war of Pharsalus, as if the river were attempting to avert the murder of Pompey by a sort of portent. (auctus per puteos mensurae notis deprehenduntur. iustum incrementum est cubitorum XVI. minores aquae non omnia rigant, ampliores detinent tardius recedendo. hae serendi tempora absumunt solo madente, illae non dant sitiente. utrumque reputat provincia. in XII cubitis famem sentit, in XIII etiamnum esurit, XIIII cubita hilaritatem adferunt, XV securitatem, XVI delicias. maximum incrementum ad hoc aevi fuit cubitorum XVIII Claudio principe, minimum V Pharsalico bello, veluti necem Magni prodigio quodam flumine adversante.)[173]

In another place, Pliny confirms the above observations more tersely:

---

[173] Pliny, *Natural History* 5.58 § 262-63.

If it has not risen more than 18 feet, there is certain to be a famine, and likewise if it has exceeded 24 feet; for it retires more slowly in proportion as it has risen in greater flood, and prevents the sowing of seed. (si XII cubita non excessit, fames certa est, nec minus si XVI exsuperavit; tanto enim tardius decedit quanto abundantius crevit, et sementem arcet.)[174]

Two important observations concerning the Nile are noted by Pliny. His studies reveal that 1) an excess of 24 feet is harmful to cultivation; and 2) the extreme measure of 27 feet was reached during the time of Claudius. The soil is flooded and much too wet at such a high point and thus the local farmers must wait until the water resides. This would have affected grain production and supply, leading to price increases.

Elsewhere, the famines that hit Judea are especially relevant, since Luke relates that a relief fund from Antioch was sent to Jerusalem (Acts 11:29-30; 12:25). During these difficult times, a benefactor named Queen Helena from Adiabeni and her son contributed considerably to the city. Josephus writes concerning them:

> Her arrival was very advantageous for the people of Jerusalem, for at that time the city was hard pressed by famine and many were perishing from want of money to purchase what they needed. Queen Helena sent some of her attendants to Alexandria to buy grain for large sums and others to Cyprus to bring back a cargo of dried figs. Her attendants speedily returned with these provisions, which she thereupon distributed among the needy. She has thus left a very great name that will be

---

[174]Ibid., 18.168 § 294-95.

famous forever among our whole people for her benefaction. When her son Izates learned of the famine, he likewise sent a great sum of money to leaders of the Jerusalemites. The distribution of this fund to the needy delivered many from the extremely severe pressure of famine. But I shall leave to a later time the further tale of good deeds performed for our city by this royal pair.[175]

According to Josephus, the famine conditions that are described above lasted throughout the reign of Tiberius Alexander, who ruled Judea from 46-48 AD.[176] Joachim Jeremias notes that the famine conditions for Jews in Jerusalem would have been exacerbated since 47/48 AD was a sabbatical year.[177] Agabus, from

---

[175]Josephus, *Jewish Antiquities* 20.51-53 § 26-29. Orosius also considered the famine severe, describing it as "fames grauissima." He writes: "In the same year of the reign of this emperor, a most serious famine took place throughout Syria which the prophets also had foretold; but Helena, the queen of the Adiabeni, a convert to the faith of Christ, ministered most generously to the needs of the Christians in Jerusalem by importing grain from Egypt." (Eodem anno imperii eius fames grauissima per Syriam facta est, quam etiam prophetae praenuntiauerant; sed Christianorum necessitatibus apud Hierosolymam conuectis ab Aegypto frumentis Helena Adiabenorum regina conuersa ad fidem Christi largissime ministrauit.) Orosius, *History* 7.6.12; Roy J. Deferrari, trans. *Paulus Orosius: The Seven Books of History Against the Pagans* (Washington, Catholic University of America Press, 1964) 297.

[176]How one dates the inception of the famine in Judea depends on which reading one accepts: 1) "upon this time" or 2) "at these times." The reading from Epitome prefers the former, while the manuscript preferred the former. If "at these times" is the proper reading, the famine could have begun during the reign of Fadus, in AD 45, since the previous sentence describes both Fadus and Tiberius Alexander. See discussions in Josephus, *Jewish Antiquities* 20.100-01 § 54-55; Kirsopp Lake, "The Chronology of Acts," *Beginnings of Christianity: Part I: The Acts of the Apostles* (ed. F. J. Foakes Jackson and Kirsopp Lake; 5 vols.; Grand Rapids: Baker, 1979) 5:452-55.

[177]Joachim Jeremias, "Sabbathjahr und neutestamentliche Chronologie," *ZNW* (1928) 98-103.

Jerusalem himself, would have benefited from the donation of Antiochene believers (Acts 11:27-30).

Before the end of Claudius' reign the famine also affects Greece in 49 AD. Eusebius records, "A famine having occurred in Greece, a bushel of wheat was sold for six drachmas." (Fame facta in Graecia, modius sex drachmis venundatus est.)[178] The exorbitant prices affected Greece as they did Egypt.

Eventually, by the end of Claudius' reign, the famine conditions were once again intense at Rome. In fact, the state of Rome was considerably worse than the early part of the decade, partly due to the dependence of the empire on foreign cargo. Tacitus describes the ordeals during the latter part of Claudius' reign:

"Many prodigies occurred during the year. Ominous birds took their seat on the Capitol; houses were overturned by repeated shocks of earthquake, and, as the panic spread, the weak were trampled underfoot in the trepidation of the crowd. A shortage of corn, grain, and the famine which resulted, were construed as a supernatural warning...It was established that the capital had provisions for fifteen days, no more; and the crisis was relieved only by the especial grace of the gods and the mildness of the winter. And yet, Heaven knows, in the past, Italy exported supplies for the legions into remote provinces; nor is sterility the trouble now, but we cultivate Africa and Egypt by preference, and the life of the Roman nation has been staked upon cargo-boats and accidents." (Multa eo anno prodigia evenere.

---

[178]Jerome, *Chronicle*, 263. Jerome translates Eusebius. Roger Pearse, trans. *Chronicles of St. Jerome*, n.p. [cited 14 January 2010]. Online: http://tiny.cc/ryq5ry; Roger Pearse, *Chronicles of St. Jerome*. n.p. [cited 14 January 2010]. Online: http://tiny.cc/9yq5ry.

Insessum diris avibus Capitolium, crebris terrae motibus prorutae domus, ac dum latius metuitur, trepidatione vulgi invalidus quisque obtriti; frugum quoque egestas et orta ex eo fames in prodigium accipiebatur...Quindecim dierum alimenta urbi, non amplius superfuisse constitit, magnaque deum benignitate et modestia hiemis rebus extremis subventum. At hercule olim Italia legionibus longinquas in provincias commeatus portabat, nec nunc infecunditate laboratur, sed Africam potius et Aegyptum exercemus, navibusque et casibus vita populi Romani permissa est.)[179]

As expected, Claudius became unpopular with the citizens of Rome because the grain is scarce. Suetonius writes concerning a public humiliation of the Caesar:

"When there was a scarcity of grain because of long-continued droughts, he was once stopped in the middle of the Forum by a mob and so pelted with abuse and at the same time with pieces of bread, that he was barely able to make his escape to the Palace by a back door; and after this experience he resorted to every possible means to bring grain to Rome, even in the winter season." (Artiore autem annona ob assiduas sterilitates detentus quondam medio Foro a turba conviciisque et simul fragminibus panis ita infestatus, ut aegre nec nisi postico evadere in Palatium valuerit, nihil non excogitavit ad invehendos etiam tempore hiberno commeatus.)[180]

The phrase "assiduas sterilitates" refers to the persistent or constant barrenness of the land that affected

---

[179]Tacitus, *Annals* 12.43 § 376-77.
[180]Suetonius, *The Lives of the Caesars* 18.2 § 36-37.

grain. In his own account, Orosius adds that this famine condition and public disgrace took place in the tenth year of Claudius reign.[181] A short time later, Claudius was poisoned to death.[182]

Thus, the reign of Claudius began and ended with famines in Rome. In between those times, famines struck Egypt, Judea, Syria, and Greece. Inflated grain prices affect most of the major areas of the Roman Empire.

### Relationship between local famines

Do the various famine accounts amount to an accurate fulfillment of Agabus' prophecy? Are the individual famines in different regions connected? Can these individual shortages be construed as one unified and universal "great famine" (λιμὸν μεγάλην) (Acts 11:28)? Is Agabus generally correct in his prophecy, but incorrect in details, as Grudem and others suggest? Some, like Bruce, support the idea that the various famines amount to a universal famine predicted by Agabus.[183] Others, like F. J. Foakes-Jackson, reject such piecemeal methods.[184]

---

[181]After describing the expulsion of Jews from Rome in the ninth year, Orosius writes: "But in the following year, so great a famine took place at Rome that the emperor, in the middle of the Forum, was taunted with reproaches by the people and most disgracefully pelted with pieces of bread; he escaped the fury of the excited people by fleeing with difficulty through a secret passage into the Palace. (Verumtamen sequenti anno tanta fames Romae fuit, ut medio foro imperator correptus a populo conuiciis et fragminibus panis turpissime infestatus, aegre per pseudothyrum in Palatium refugiens furorem excitatae plebis euaserit.) Orosius, *History* 7.6.17; Deferrari, trans. *Paulus Orosius: The Seven Books of History Against the Pagans*, 297.

[182]Orosius, *History* 7.6.18.

[183]Bruce, *The Acts of the Apostles*, 276; Harrison, *Acts*, 186; Marshall, *The Acts of the Apostles*, 204; Kistemaker, *Acts*, 425; Williams, *Acts*, 206.

[184]F. J. Foakes-Jackson, *The Acts of the Apostles* (Moffatt New Testament Commentary; London: Hodder & Stoughton, 1951) 102;

Yet another camp has supported a theory of the aforementioned Kenneth S. Gapp.[185] Gapp proposes that the famine of Agabus is universal based on socio-economic reasons. He begins by establishing that famines in the ancient and modern world are essentially "class famines" that cause starvation among the poor, while the rich rely on their reserves of money and grain.[186] In other words, famines do not necessarily cause universal hunger, though every strata of the society faces hardship. The actual reason for the universal hardship during famines is the general rise in prices. Thus, rather than focusing on the failure of crop, the rise of prices is more essential to famines.[187]

An entire nation or an empire that rely on import of grain could face huge fluctuations in prices if the few exporting countries suffer harvest failures. Indeed, the Roman empire of Claudius is characterized by heavy dependence on Egyptian imports, as witnessed by secular sources.[188] Also, as explained above, papyri from Tebtunis and Pliny the Elder confirm that Egypt faced unprecedented famines and price increases during Claudius' reign. Gapp explains:

---

Rackham, *The Acts of the Apostles*, 172-73; Conzelmann, *The Acts of the Apostles*, 90; Haenchen, *The Acts of the Apostles*, 374.

[185]Witherington III, *The Acts of the Apostles*, 372-73; Fitzmeyer, *The Acts of the Apostles*, 481.

[186]Gapp, "The Universal Famine under Claudius," 261.

[187]Ibid., 261-62.

[188]Tacitus recounts: "And yet, Heaven knows, in the past, Italy exported supplies for the legions into remote provinces; nor is sterility the trouble now, but we cultivate Africa and Egypt by preference, and the life of the Roman nation has been staked upon cargo-boats and accidents." (At hercule olim Italia legionibus longinquas in provincias commeatus portabat, nec nunc infecunditate laboratur, sed Africam potius et Aegyptum exercemus, navibusque et casibus vita populi Romani permissa est.) Tacitus, *Annals* 12.43 § 376-77. See also Dio Cassius, *Dio's Roman History* 60.11.1-2 § 392-93.

Now a failure of the harvest in one or two lands might easily affect the price of grain in the whole Mediterranean world. The failure of the afflicted countries to export grain, and perhaps even the necessity of transporting grain to supply their needs, would certainly have some effect upon all the markets of the Roman world. This was particularly true if Egypt suffered from scarcity, for this country ordinarily exported enormous quantities of grain.[189]

In conclusion, Gapp makes an insightful and calculated contribution to the proper understanding of "famine" and how a shortage of grain in Egypt led to a universal famine. Since several secular sources support Gapp's theory, his view best explains how the famine prophesied by Agabus can be universal. Thus, Agabus is justified not only by Luke, but various Greco-Roman sources.

*Summary*

Thus both Luke and Greco-Roman sources suggest that there was indeed a universal famine during the reign of Claudius. The narrative of Acts, written by Luke, confirms the fulfillment of the prophecy and the acceptance of Agabus as a genuine prophet. The various Greco-Roman sources substantiate the view that the famine prophecy is accurate. The prices of grain increased in many different regions of the Roman Empire, because of the shortage of grain in Egypt, an important exporting country.

---

[189]Gapp, "The Universal Famine under Claudius," 262.

## Conclusion

This chapter dealt with the nature of the famine prophecy and its fulfillment. The nature of Agabus' prophecy is largely revealed in the word studies of ἐσήμανεν (signified), διὰ τοῦ πνεύματος (through the Spirit), and ἐφ' ὅλην τὴν οἰκουμένην (upon the whole world). The prophecy is a clear, divine speech that pertains to the entire Roman Empire.

The fulfillment of the prophecy is primarily confirmed by Luke and secondarily supported by Greco-Roman sources. Luke recounts that the prophecy was fulfilled during the reign of Claudius (Acts 11:28). Agabus is later accepted into the congregation of Caesarea (Acts 21:10-14). Greco-Roman sources reveal famine conditions throughout the Roman Empire which stem from price increases of imports. Egypt, the major exporting source of grain to the Roman world, faced cataclysmically high water levels that limited grain production. The resulting conditions reveal an accurate fulfillment of Agabus' prophecy.

# CHAPTER IV

# IMPRISONMENT PROPHECY OF AGABUS

## Introduction

Much time has elapsed since the famine prophecy of Agabus.[190] The teacher, Saul of Antioch, is now the missionary, Paul, the founder of many churches. Now he is determined to expand his influence into new regions such as Rome. However, the apostle must first go to Jerusalem.[191] Along the way, there are divine warnings that culminate in Caesarea, where Paul and his companions stay at the home of Philip the evangelist (Acts 21:8). In Caesarea, Paul is told the pending consequence of his plans.

Agabus arrives alone from Judea with a message concerning Paul (Acts 21:10). The message of Agabus is not only a verbal message, but also a symbolic act (Acts 21:11). Luke records: καὶ ἐλθὼν πρὸς ἡμᾶς καὶ ἄρας τὴν ζώνην τοῦ Παύλου δήσας ἑαυτοῦ τοὺς πόδας καὶ τὰς χεῖρας (And after coming to us and taking the belt of Paul, binding himself his feet and hands). This dramatic

---

[190]Though the issue of chronology is not as critical as the previous prophecy, the date of the second prophecy is still worth noting. Paul probably arrived in Caesarea in 57 AD, on the seventh week after Passover. Riesner, *Paul's Early Period*, 322; Kistemaker, *Acts*, 749.

[191]For further studies on divine direction in Paul's life, see Charles H. Cosgrave, "The Divine Dei in Luke-Acts: Investigations into the Lukan Understanding of God's Providence." *Novum Testamentum* 26 (1984) 168-90.

act is accompanied by the prophetic utterance: εἶπεν· Τάδε λέγει τὸ πνεῦμα τὸ ἅγιον Τὸν ἄνδρα οὗ ἐστιν ἡ ζώνη αὕτη, οὕτως δήσουσιν ἐν Ἰερουσαλὴμ οἱ Ἰουδαῖοι καὶ παραδώσουσιν εἰς χεῖρας ἐθνῶν (he said, "Thus says the Holy Spirit: In this manner the Jews will bind the man to whom belongs this belt and they will hand him over into the hands of the Gentiles").

The prophecy of Acts 21:10-11 has important similarities and differences from the famine prophecy of Acts 11:28. Three differences are notable. While the famine prophecy is grand in scale, dealing with the entire Roman Empire, the later prophecy deals with a single person and his future circumstances in Jerusalem. Secondly, while the famine prophecy is recorded by Luke in a summary format, the author preserves the words of Agabus in this second account. Thus, one has at hand the only specific genuine NT prophetic material from a NT prophet. This is a rare find, since most NT prophecies are from apostles, not prophets. Lastly, Luke explicitly narrates that the famine prophecy is fulfilled but there is no similarly explicit statement in regard to the imprisonment prophecy.

The similarities are also important. Both are prophecies of Agabus proclaimed in the midst of a congregation. Both are given when Paul is present. Both are sourced in the Holy Spirit.

Most importantly, the same questions can be asked concerning the level of accuracy. In order to analyze the accuracy of the foretelling accuracy of the imprisonment prophecy, a careful study of Agabus' symbolic act and his words must be undertaken. After gaining an understanding of the nature of the imprisonment prophecy, the narratives of Acts will be perused to confirm whether Agabus is accurate in the details of his prophecy.

## Nature of the Imprisonment Prophecy

Four major components of Agabus' second prophecy are worth examining: 1) the symbolic act; 2) the citation, τάδε λέγει τὸ πνεῦμα τὸ ἅγιον (Thus says the Holy Spirit); 3) the binding, δήσουσιν ἐν Ἰερουσαλὴμ οἱ Ἰουδαῖοι (The Jews will bind in Jerusalem); and 4) the transfer, παραδώσουσιν εἰς χεῖρας ἐθνῶν (will deliver into the hands of the Gentiles). A thorough understanding of these elements is essential to evaluating the foretelling accuracy of Agabus.

### *The symbolic act: analysis of the prophetic act*

Acts 21:10 describes the prophetic act of Agabus. Luke records: καὶ ἐλθὼν πρὸς ἡμᾶς καὶ ἄρας τὴν ζώνην τοῦ Παύλου δήσας ἑαυτοῦ τοὺς πόδας καὶ τὰς χεῖρας (And after coming to us and taking the belt of Paul, binding himself feet and hands) (Acts 21:11). Robertson notes that the three aorist participles in succession vividly portray the dramatic act.[192] The belt used in this act is probably a long strip belt, wrapped around the body several times and used to hold money.[193] The binding process leaves Agabus unable to walk or move his hands freely.

Many scholars note similar dramatic actions done by OT prophets.[194] Some suggested examples include: Ahijah

---

[192]A. T. Robertson, *Acts* (Word Pictures in the New Testament; Nashville: Broadman, 1931) 364.

[193]BDAG, 431; Larkin Jr., *Acts*, 304.

[194]Stanley D. Toussaint, "Acts," *BKC* (Ed. John F. Walvoord and Roy B. Zuck; 2 vols. Wheaton: Victor, 1985) 2:415; Johannes Munck, *The Acts of the Apostles* (The Anchor Bible; Garden City, NY: Doubleday, 1967) 207; J. B. Polhill, *Acts* (New American Commentary 26; Nashville: Broadman, 1992) 435; Harrison, *Acts,* 322; Haenchen, *The Acts of the Apostles,* 602; Bruce, *The Book of Acts,* 401; Fernando, *Acts,* 552; Rackham, *The Acts of the Apostles,* 401; Witherington III, *The Acts of the Apostles,* 634; Williams, *Acts,* 362; Larkin Jr., *Acts,* 304;

with his cloak (1 Kg 11:29-39); Isaiah and Maher-Shalal-Hash-Baz (Isa 8:1-4); Isaiah, without sackcloth or sandals (Isa 20:2-4); Jeremiah with a linen belt (Jer 13:1-11); Jeremiah with a clay jar (Jer 19:1-15); Jeremiah with a yoke (Jer 27:1-22); Ezekiel with a clay tablet and an iron pan (Ezek 4:1-3); Ezekiel with his shaved hair and scales (Ezek 5:1-17); and Hosea's marriage with Gomer (Hosea 1:2). Other examples include Zechariah's crowning of Joshua the high priest (Zech 6:9-15).

Perhaps the most significant common phenomenon between the symbolic acts of the OT prophets and Agabus is the attachment of a divine message. The symbolic act of Agabus is immediately followed by a prophetic formula: τάδε λέγει τὸ πνεῦμα τὸ ἅγιον (Thus says the Holy Spirit). In the OT, the prophetic formula, "thus says the Lord" (τάδε λέγει κύριος in LXX), is found after the symbolic acts of Ahijah, Jeremiah, Ezekiel, and Zechariah (1 Kg 11:31; Jer 13:9; 19:11; Ezek 5:5, 7, 8; Zech 6:12). Thus, one can at least positively affirm that Agabus, as a NT prophet, behaves much like an authoritative OT prophet. Now his words must also be scrutinized.

*The prophetic citation: analysis of "Thus says the Holy Spirit"*

After coming to Caesarea from Judea and performing the dramatic act, Agabus speaks. His first words reveal the source of the oracle: the Holy Spirit (τὸ πνεῦμα τὸ ἅγιον). At first glance, it is apparent that the utterance from Agabus' mouth is sourced in divinity. Like the famine prophecy above, the notion that errors are blended in with inspired revelation is hardly present.

However, Grudem is not convinced that this prophetic formula introduces an accurate citation of divine speech. He observes in Ignatius' *Epistle to the*

---

Conzelmann, *The Acts of the Apostles*, 178; Fitzmeyer, *The Acts of the Apostles*, 689.

*Philadelphians* and *The Epistle of Barnabas* that "the phrase hardly introduces a direct quotation" and most instances of the phrase often "introduce extremely free paraphrases with interpretation of the Old Testament" (Ign. *Phld.* 7:1-2; *Barn.* 6:8; 9:2).[195] Then, Grudem concludes:

> "Thus says the Holy Spirit" means here not that the very words of the prophecy were from the Holy Spirit but only that the content generally had been revealed by the Spirit. In this case Acts 21:10-11 would fit the pattern of prophecy in 1 Corinthians...It is clearly possible, therefore, that Agabus's introductory statement meant nothing more to him than, "This is generally (or approximately) what the Holy Spirit is saying to us."[196]

However, the sample that Grudem uses is quite small. He cites five verses from the apostolic fathers.[197] He realizes the need to evaluate the many verses in the LXX. He is cognizant of the large number of verses where the phrase Τάδε λέγει τὸ πνεῦμα τὸ ἅγιον (Thus says the Holy Spirit) introduces direct quotations from God. Still, Grudem defends his conclusions above:

> The problem with this solution is that this phrase, Greek *tade legei*, is used frequently in the Greek translation of the Old Testament (the Septuagint) to introduce the words of the Lord in the Old Testament prophets ("Thus says the

---

[195] Ign. *Phld.* 7:1-2; *Barn.* 9:2; Grudem, *The Gift of Prophecy in the New Testament and Today*, 82.

[196] Ibid.

[197] Ign. *Phld.* 7:1-2; *Barn.* 6:8; 9:2, 5. The date of the *Letters of Ignatius* is estimated to be near AD 110, while the date of *The Epistle of Barnabas* ranges from AD 70 to 132. *The Apostolic Fathers* (Trans. by J. B. Lightfoot and J. R. Harmer; Edited and Revised by Michael W. Holmes; Second Edition; Grand Rapids: Baker, 1989) 82, 160.

Lord..."). On the other hand, it is also used to introduce statements from many other people, not always with direct quotations, so perhaps it need not always signify that the actual words of the person quoted would follow. Moreover, the exact words used by Agabus, "Thus says the Holy Spirit," are never elsewhere used to introduce Scripture or Old Testament prophetic speech which consisted of the very words of God.[198]

Whether Grudem is correct in evaluating the phrase in this manner remains to be seen after a more thorough investigation than the one he undertakes. A word study of τάδε λέγει (Thus says) may reveal much about whether the phrase allows loose interpretations or direct citations.

### "Thus says" in LXX

How the formula used by Agabus compares with the OT formula is an important study. The phrase "thus says" (τάδε paired with λέγει or a similar speech verb in Greek, most commonly translated from "thus says" in Hebrew) appears 382 times in the LXX, and the subject is God or another authoritative figure in the majority of the cases.[199] When OT prophets use the formula with

---

[198]Grudem, *The Gift of Prophecy in the New Testament and Today*, 82-83. Grudem overlooks the importance of Hebrews 3:7. The syntax of Hebrews 3:7 closely resembles Acts 21:11. The phrase λέγει τὸ πνεῦμα τὸ ἅγιον (says the Holy Spirit) is found, except that καθὼς is used instead of τάδε. The phrase introduces the inspired speech of Psalm 95:7-11. So then, the force of Grudem's argument wholly rests on his view of τάδε.

[199]God is the subject in every case except 41 times. In 39 instances where God is not the subject, a ruler or a person in formal authority is the subject. The list of rulers, people, or corporations in authority include: Joseph (Gen 45:9); Pharaoh (Exo 5:10); representative voice of the entire nation of Israel (Num 20:14; Josh 22:16); Balak (Num 22:16); Jephthah (Jdg(A) 11:15); a Levite man to his messengers (Jdg(A) 19:30); Saul's army to messengers (1 Sam 11:9); representative voice of the

YHWH, they introduce a direct speech from God. Aune observes:

> Israelite prophets frequently used the so-called messenger formula "thus says Yahweh" to introduce oracular speeches...In the OT the prophetic use of the messenger formula indicates a consciousness of the divine origin and authority of the message, and it is always Yahweh who speaks in the first person following the formula.[200]

It is also helpful to view how τάδε (thus) is used with other words. The pronoun is found either with a non-speech verb, modifying noun, or alone 71 times. In twelve verses, a pair of the pronouns is combined with two optative aorist verbs to form an oath formula: "May (he) do to me...and more." In each of these twelve verses, the subject is the God of Israel or some foreign deity. [201] Saul also employs a similar formula, but with a single τάδε (thus) he regards himself as the executer of the oath (1 Sam 11:7). In twelve other instances, its independent case form is used to translate "behold." The

---

Philistines (1 Sam 14:9-10); Saul (1 Sam 18:25; 20:7); Jonathan to a youth (1 Sam 20:22); David (1 Sam 25:6; 2 Sam 11:25); Solomon (1 Kg 2:30); Joab (1 Kg 2:30 (2)); Ben-Hadad (1 Kg 21:3, 5); Ahaziah (2 Kg 1:11); Joram (2 Kg 9:18, 19); Rehoboam (2 Kg 12:10 (2)); Sennecherib (2 Kg 18:19, 29, 31; Isa 36:4, 16); Hezekiah (2 Kg 19:3; Isa 37:3); Prophet Amos (Amos 7:11); Cyrus (2 Chron 36:23; 1 Esdras 2:2); Prophet Ieremias (2 Macc 15:15); King Ptolemy (3 Macc 5:3); royal family of Ptolemy (3 Macc 5:39); Eleazaros the priest (3 Macc 6:1). At minimum, the phrase seems to be reserved for the citation of authoritative figures, if not divinity. See also Josephus, *Jewish Antiquities* 11.26 § 326-27.

[200]Aune, *Prophecy in Early Christianity and the Ancient Mediterranean World*, 89.

[201]Those who refer to the God of Israel as the subject in the oath formula are: Ruth (Ruth 1:17); Eli (1 Sam 3:17) ; Saul (1 Sam 14:44); Jonathan (1 Sam 20:13); David (1 Sam 25:22; 2 Sam 3:35; 2 Sam 19:14); Aber (2 Sam 3:9); Solomon (1 Kg 2:23); King of Israel (2 Kg 6:31). Those who refer to foreign deities in the oath formula are Jezebel (1 Kgb 19:2) and Ben-hadad (1Kg 21:10).

pronoun is used as a demonstrative or an adjectival pronoun in twenty-five more instances. Finally, the remaining nine instances refer to the actions or the writings of leaders, high-standing officials, or the contents of formal records.[202]

So far, it is readily apparent that τάδε (thus) is used most often to cite authoritative figures or documents. This usage makes up the majority of the cases in the LXX. In 380 out of the 382 instances, τάδε (thus), combined with a speech verb, is used to describe a speech act of someone of higher authority. Based on OT data alone, one can agree with Wallace, Culy, and Parson that there is a strong sense of solemnity that accompanies the pronoun.[203] There is also a strong indication of an accurate citation.

*"Thus says" in NT*

τάδε (thus) occurs in various forms ten times in the NT. The phrase in discussion, τάδε λέγει (thus says), occurs seven times in Revelation 2-3, with Christ as the subject in each instance.[204] In Luke 10:39, the pronoun in different case and gender, is used to introduce Mary, the sister of Martha. In James 4:13, the pronoun is used adjectivally to describe a city.

---

[202] The remaining instances where "thus" is combined with a non-speech verb are: 1) sons of Eli (1 Sam 2:14); 2) royal archives (1 Esdras 6:22); 3) Rehum the commander, Shimshai the scribe, and other officials (Ezra 4:9); 4) a letter to king Darius from Tattenai the governor, Shethar-bozenai and other officials (Ezra 5:7); Artaxerxes (Est 3:13); Leukios, an official (1 Macc 15:15).

[203] Daniel A. Wallace, *Greek Grammar Beyond the Basics: An Exegetical Syntax of the*
*New Testament* (Grand Rapids: Zondervan, 1996) 328; Martin M. Culy and Mikeal C. Parsons, *Acts: A Handbook on the Greek Text* (Waco: Baylor University Press, 2003) 405.

[204] Rev 2:1, 8, 12, 18; 3:1, 7, 14.

Though the sample size in the NT is considerably smaller than the instances in the OT, the usage of the pronoun in the NT is quite similar. The majority of the NT usages signify divine speech. Eight out of ten instances describe the utterances of God, albeit the NT records the words of the second and third persons of the Trinity (Acts 21:11; Rev 2-3). So then both in the LXX and the NT, τάδε λέγει (thus says) is used to describe divine speech, either from the Father, Christ or the Holy Spirit in the overwhelming majority of cases.

*"Thus says" in church fathers*

Though only a few verses employ a form of this pronoun, the church fathers must also be perused, since Grudem relies on them heavily. The pronoun is found in seven different instances.[205] In 1 Clement 12:4, the pronoun is used independently as a referent to Rahab in Jericho. In the rest of 1 Clement, the pronoun is used adjectivally to describe the present day and the letter itself (*1 Clem.* 50:3; 63:2).

The four other instances are of considerable interest, since one finds therein τάδε (thus) and a form of λέγω (say). All three verses in Barnabas relate to what God says (*Barn.* 6:8; 9:2, 5). Admittedly, as Grudem contends, there are only loose citations of OT passages, though one may not agree with him that they are "extremely free paraphrases."[206] Grudem is also correct concerning Ignatius. In *Ignatius to the Philadelphians*, there is a discrepancy between the delivery of a prophetic word and the revelation received (Ign. *Phld.* 7:2 c.f. 7:1).[207]

---

[205] *1 Clem.* 12:4; 50:3; 63:2; *Barn.* 6:8; 9:2, 5; Ign. *Phld.* 7:2.

[206] Grudem, *The Gift of Prophecy in the New Testament and Today*, 82.

[207] Grudem appears to accept 7:2 as Ignatius' elaboration of the actual prophecy in 7:1. His argument turns on this premise. However, a case can be made for just the opposite; 7:1 is the actual elaboration of 7:2. If the latter is the case, the second verse which employs τάδε λέγει

From the church fathers alone, Grudem can make a case for his view that "thus says" introduce loose interpretations. However, one may question whether the uninspired writings can sustain the weight of his argument.[208]

*"Thus says" in Acts 21:11*

The issue at hand concerns whether one can agree with Grudem that there is no imperative on the part of Agabus to quote the Holy Spirit verbatim when he uses the formula.[209] In other words, does the construction τάδε λέγει (thus says) in Acts 21:11 demand an accurate quotation?

Prophetic figures of both the LXX and the NT utilize the formula in discussion to introduce divine speech. Admittedly, there are some exceptions among the church fathers. However, the church fathers are merely referring to prophecy, not prophesying. Furthermore, the church fathers are not inspired writings on par with the Scriptures or NT prophecy. Most of the church fathers were excluded from serious considerations of canonicity, even in the early days of the church.[210] One must evaluate their writings accordingly.

---

(thus says) can no longer be substantiated as an announcement of a loose interpretation. Ibid.

[208]Grudem is inconsistent in his evaluation of the early church writings. On one hand, he relies on these letters to support his views concerning "thus says," while on the other hand, he conveniently dismisses the *Didache* when it supports the infallible NT prophecy view. Ibid., 87-88.

[209]The fact that Acts 21:11 is the only verse where the Holy Spirit is the subject of the prophetic formula does not invalidate the phrase as an acceptable introduction to direct words of God. If the Holy Spirit is divine, then His words would be just as divine as the other persons in the Trinity. Ibid., 83.

[210]See discussions of the Muratorian Canon (2nd century) and Eusebius' *Ecclesiastical History* (4th century): Bruce M. Metzger, *The Canon of the New Testament: Its Origin, Development, and Significance*

It is safe to assume that both the OT prophets and the NT prophets, such as Agabus, are faithful to the word which they cite. Grudem has neglected to present the hundreds of instances in the Scriptures where τάδε λέγει (thus says) is used in this manner. He bases his position on scant evidence from the church fathers and opposes the force of Agabus' prophetic formula, which is rooted in the OT prophets.[211]

*The binding: analysis of "bind"*

Agabus, after citing the Holy Spirit, relays the message of Paul's imprisonment: δήσουσιν ἐν Ἰερουσαλὴμ οἱ Ἰουδαῖοι (The Jews will bind in Jerusalem). Paul is clearly τὸν ἄνδρα οὗ ἐστιν ἡ ζώνη αὕτη (the man whose belt is this), so the apostle is the one to be bound. The manner in which Paul is bound is indicated by οὕτως (in this manner). Paul will be bound physically by the Jews in Jerusalem with no way of escape with his hands and feet. The figurative binding is not suggested here.[212]

*The transfer: analysis of "deliver"*

Paul's ordeals do not end with the binding. The Jews will hand over Paul into the hands of the Gentiles (παραδώσουσιν εἰς χεῖρας ἐθνῶν). The prophecy here appears simple enough. The Jews bind Paul, but the Gentiles end up with him.

However, one issue must be taken up concerning the verb. Grudem introduces a thought concerning παραδίδωμι (deliver) that is germane to the current discussion. According to Grudem, the subject of the verb

---

(Oxford: Clarendon Press, 1997) 191-207.

[211]Haenchen, *The Acts of the Apostles*, 602; Williams, *Acts*, 362; Marshall, *The Acts of the Apostles*, 340; Fitzmeyer, *The Acts of the Apostles*, 689.

[212]For figurative usages of "bind" in NT, see Matt 16:19 (2); 18:18 (2); Luke 13:16; Acts 20:22; Rom 7:2; 1 Cor 7:27, 39; Rev 9:14; 20:2.

must always be "actively, willingly, and consciously" performing the act. He writes:

> Here the Greek word for deliver is *paradidōmi*, "to deliver, hand over." Essential to the sense of this word is the idea of actively, consciously, willingly "delivering, giving over, handing over" something or someone to someone (or something) else—this is the case in all of the other 119 instances of its use in the New Testament.[213]

This volitional idea is quite important in understanding this prophecy. In Acts 21:32-33, Paul is taken forcibly from the mob of Jews in Jerusalem. If Grudem is correct and volition is absolutely essential to this verb, the Jews do not essentially "hand over" Paul.

One can agree that such consciousness is implicit in the verb, but to say that it is "essential" is another thing. Such an "essential" idea is not indicated in the standard lexicons or dictionaries, nor is the nuance found in every case of the 119 instances.[214] In Mark 4:29, the subject of this verb is "crop," hardly something that can "actively, consciously, willingly" deliver!

In fact, certain verbs, though usually accompanied by volition, can have exceptions where the subject does not "actively, consciously, and willingly" perform it. For example, in John 11:49-52, Caiaphas the high priest unwittingly prophesies while rebuking the council of chief priests and Pharisees. John narrates the ironic scene: τοῦτο δὲ ἀφ' ἑαυτοῦ οὐκ εἶπεν (but he did not speak this from himself) (John 11:51). Caiaphas'

---

[213] Grudem, *The Gift of Prophecy in the New Testament and Today*, 78.

[214] BDAG, 761-63; MM, 482-83; Friedrich Büchsel, "παραδίδωμι," *TDNT* 2 (1964) 169-72; Wiard Popkes, "παραδίδωμι," *Exegetical Dictionary of the New Testament* 3 (1990) 18-20.

malicious remarks become a prophecy, even though he does not "actively, consciously, and willingly" do so.[215]

Perhaps the most telling evidence against Grudem's view of this verb comes from Paul himself. In Acts 28:17, Paul testifies, παρεδόθην εἰς τὰς χεῖρας τῶν Ῥωμαίων (I was delivered into the hands of the Romans). In every instance of Jewish contact with Paul in Jerusalem, they desire to exterminate Paul (Acts 21:31; 22:22; 23:10, 12).[216] However, Paul comments that he was delivered over in spite of this deadly maliciousness. In other words, the Jews "delivered" Paul regardless of the intent.

Thus, a verb does not necessarily require volition on the part of its subject. One cannot substantiate the view that the Jews must consciously "deliver" Paul to be accurate. Such volition is not essential to the meaning of the verb.

*Summary*

The analyses of Agabus' second prophecy lead to the following conclusions: 1) Paul will be physically bound; 2) the Holy Spirit is cited as the source of the prophecy; 3) Paul will be bound by the Jews; and 4) Paul will be handed over by the Jews to the Gentiles. Agabus acts and speaks like an OT prophet, with the authority of the Holy Spirit. This prophecy will occur, regardless of the will of man. With the exact words of Agabus under

---

[215]A. T. Robertson, *John/Hebrews* (Word Pictures in the New Testament; 6 vols; Nashville: Broadman, 1930) 209.

[216]Grudem's argument that this "deliverance" took place from Jerusalem into the Roman judicial system ignores the context of Acts 28:17, in which Paul says just before: οὐδὲν ἐναντίον ποιήσας τῷ λαῷ ἢ τοῖς ἔθεσι τοῖς πατρῴοις (Though I have done nothing against the people or the customs of the fathers...). Clearly, the ones "delivering" are the Jews of Jerusalem and Paul is taken out of their hands in Acts 21:33 and does not fall prey to them again. Grudem, *The Gift of Prophecy in the New Testament and Today*, 310.

scrutiny, one can make conclusions concerning the foretelling accuracy of Agabus. [217]

## Fulfillment of the Prophecy

With the important portions of the imprisonment prophecy analyzed, the prophecy can be evaluated with regard to its accuracy. Three different views are present for discussion and assessment of its fulfillment: 1) general fulfillment view; 2) causative fulfillment view; and 3) assumed fulfillment view. After assessing the critical issues that arise with each view, the preferred view will be selected.

### General Fulfillment View

Those who take this view discredit the details of Agabus' imprisonment prophecy but accept that the NT prophet was generally correct. Proponents of the fallible NT prophecy view accept this view of Acts 21:10-11.[218] Grudem is a fitting representative. He writes:

> It is not that Agabus has spoken in a totally false or a misleading way; it is just that

---

[217] It is also worth noting that there are significant parallels between Luke's account of Jesus' ministry and Paul's. For example, W. Radl notes that the various prophecies of suffering characterize both ministries: Acts 20:22-25; 21:4, 10-12/Luke 9:22, 44f.; 12:50; 13:32f.; 17:25; 18:31-34. However, Radl suspects that Luke redacted, modified, or created accounts freely at the cost of historicity. Marshall, on the other hand, maintains that Luke is historically accurate while accepting the parallels between Christ and Paul. W. Radl, *Paulus und Jesus im lukanischen Doppelwerk: Untersuchungen zu Parallelmotiven im Lukasevangelium und in der Apostelgeschichte* (Bern: H. Lang/Frankfurt: P. Lang, 1975); I. Howard Marshall, "Acts and the 'Former Treatise,'" *The Book of Acts in Its Ancient Literary Setting* (ed. Bruce W. Winter and Andrew D. Clarke; The Book of Acts in Its First Century Setting 1; Grand Rapids: Eerdmans, 1993) 180-82.

[218] Carson, *Showing the Spirit*, 97-98; Witherington III, *The Acts of the Apostles*, 634; Barret, *A Critical and Exegetical Commentary on the Acts of the Apostles*, 2:995.

he has the details wrong. But this kind of minor inaccuracy is exactly compatible with the type of prophecy we found earlier in 1 Corinthians, in which the prophet receives some kind of revelation and then reports it in his own words. He would have the general idea correct (Paul would be imprisoned at Jerusalem), but the details somewhat wrong...It seems...that the best solution is to say that Agabus had a "revelation" from the Holy Spirit concerning what would happen to Paul in Jersualem, and gave a prophecy which included his own interpretation of this revelation (and therefore some mistakes in the exact details). Luke then recorded Agabus' prophecy exactly, and recorded the subsequent events exactly, even including those aspects of the events which showed Agabus to be slightly wrong at some points.[219]

Without incriminating Agabus as a false prophet, Grudem advances his view that NT prophecy can be inaccurate in details yet generally correct. There are two details in which Agabus is allegedly incorrect. First, it was not the Jews who eventually bound Paul at Jerusalem as Agabus predicted, but the Romans (Acts 21:33; 22:29).[220] Secondly, Jews did not deliver Paul into the hands of Romans, but out of zeal attempted to take his life.[221] In spite of these mistakes, Agabus is correct that Paul would be imprisoned in Jerusalem. Thus Agabus' imprisonment prophecy is generally correct.

However, there are three serious issues which must be dealt with if one accepts this view: 1) inspiration and

---

[219]Grudem, *The Gift of Prophecy in the New Testament and Today*, 78-79.
[220]Ibid., 78.
[221]Ibid.

inerrancy; 2) verbal correspondence; and 3) the essence of Acts 21:11. Each issue will be discussed next.

*Inspiration and inerrancy*

The first issue with this view concerns the inspiration and the infallbility of the Holy Spirit. If one follows Grudem's view, the Holy Spirit is the culprit of prophetic error. The word study of τάδε λέγει (thus says) revealed that the prophetic figures in the LXX and the NT often employ the phrase to introduce sayings of God. In Acts 21:11, Agabus quotes the Holy Spirit. So then, as Robert Thomas points out, one cannot avoid the unorthodox implication of Grudem's position, which leads to accusations against the Holy Spirit.[222] Thomas concludes this from his observation of "thus says," which is used to introduce utterances from the second person of the Trinity in Rev 2-3.[223] If the Holy Spirit is just as divine as the Son in Revelation and the Father in the OT, why question His accuracy?[224]

*Verbal correspondence*

Secondly, this view demands specific statements of corresponding words before confirming a prophecy. The mob scene in Acts 21:27-40 is appropriately studied, but Luke, as a narrator, does not use the same verb that Agabus used to predict the incident. Even those who

---

[222]Thomas, "Prophecy Rediscovered?," 91.

[223]Ibid.

[224]Though supporters of this view would not agree, inspiration and inerrancy are also issues that would be challenged if the logical ramifications of this view are played out. One scholar writes: "Agabus quotes the very words of the Spirit exactly as the ancient prophets did. If this is not verbal Inspiration, pray, what is? The Spirit has no difficulty whatever in communicating his words and his will to a prophet with utmost exactness; nor is there anything in the least 'mechanical' about the process, this dreadful feature which modern theologians feel they must eliminate at all hazards even though they destroy Inspiration itself." R. C. H. Lenski, *The Interpretation of the Acts of the Apostles* (Minneapolis: Augsburg Publishing House, 1934) 869.

oppose Grudem's view must admit that Luke is not explicit in this matter, but one may question whether a demand for such verbal correspondence is reasonable.²²⁵

It is apparent that considering the mob scene in Jerusalem is not enough. One must also consider the vital terms in Acts 28:17. Paul's reflection of the Jerusalem riot in Acts 28:17 is quite problematic for Grudem's view. In this verse, Paul not only confirms his bound state as a prisoner before the transfer, but he explicitly states that he was delivered into the hands of the Gentile Romans from the hands of the Jews. He testifies in Rome, stating, δέσμιος ἐξ Ἱεροσολύμων παρεδόθην εἰς τὰς χεῖρας τῶν Ῥωμαίων (I was delivered as a prisoner from Jerusalem into the hands of the Romans). This verse provides all of the fulfillment language demanded by Agabus' prophecy in Acts 21:11, because Paul's reflection of the events match in vocabulary with Agabus' prophecy. The noun δέσμιος (prisoner) is cognately and conceptually related to the verb δέω (bind). Paul considers himself a "prisoner," perhaps bound by ropes, even before the Romans arrive and place him in chains.

The verb παραδίδωμι (deliver) is found in both verses, but in different tenses. Appropriately, παραδίδωμι (deliver) is in future tense in Acts 21:11, to express prediction, but aorist passive in Acts 28:17, to express reflection of the past. In Acts 21:11, the verb παραδίδωμι (deliver) does not require volition, as stated above. Thus, even if Paul is taken forcibly out of the Jews' custody against their will, he is still "delivered."²²⁶

---

²²⁵Grudem, *The Gift of Prophecy in the New Testament and Today*, 79-80.

²²⁶See discussion above. Robert L. Thomas, "Prophecy Rediscovered? Review of The Gift of Prophecy in the New Testament and Today," *BSac* 149 (1992) 91; Oldham, "The Gift of Prophecy and Modern Revivals," 125-26.

Grudem counters by stating that Acts 28:17 is describing the transfer from the Jewish Sanhedrin at Jerusalem to the Roman court system at Caesarea (Acts 23:23-35).[227] The force of his argument is centered in the phrase ἐξ Ἱεροσολύμων (from Jerusalem).[228] However, the Sanhedrin itself is assembled under the authority of Claudius Lysias (Acts 22:30). It is clear that Lysias, the commander, has the custody of Paul, since during the mob scene and thenceforth he does not relinquish control over Paul (Acts 23:25-30). So then, the exchange of the prisoner, Paul, between Jews and Romans must take place in Acts 21:33, not during the trip to Caesarea. The phrase "from Jerusalem" simply describes the type of prisoner Paul is: a Jerusalem kind.

### Essence of the prophecy

Thirdly, based on his arguments, even Grudem cannot redeem Agabus from total failure because the so-called "minor details" are the very essence of Agabus' prophecy. Agabus provides specific supplemental, new revelation to add on to what Paul has already learned from the Holy Spirit in the past. What Agabus provides are the finer details of Paul's fate in Jerusalem.

In fact, what is "generally" true of Agabus' prophecy is already known before Paul arrives in Caesarea. Paul requests prayer from Roman believers for safe arrival in Jerusalem (Rom 15:31). Already, Paul is aware of dangers in Jerusalem. What do the subsequent events in Paul's journey reveal as he prepares to go to Jerusalem? Cunningham explains how he sees progressive revelation concerning Paul's fate in the following manner: 1) In Acts 20:23, the reader is informed that the Holy Spirit warns Paul of bonds and afflictions in every city; 2) In the penultimate passage, Acts 21:4, a short narrative

---

[227]Grudem, *Systematic Theology*, 1052-53.
[228]Ibid., 1052.

illustrates the principle of Acts 20:23 in the city of Tyre, with warnings that Jerusalem is a dangerous destiny; and 3) Finally, in Caesarea, a detailed, climactic narrative vividly reveals the perpetrators of Paul's arrest and his fate (Acts 21:10-14).[229] So then, what new revelation does Agabus provide except the specific details of Paul's arrest? Once the minor details of Agabus' prophecy, the manner of Paul's arrest and the agents are taken away, what is left besides the obvious and what is already known? Grudem himself admits this problem:

> Now it might be argued that Luke has no intention of showing that Agabus gave an inaccurate prophecy. These are really only differences in detail, someone might say. However, this explanation does not take full enough account of the fact that these are the *only* two details Agabus mentions—they are, in terms of content, the heart of his prophecy. In fact, these details are what make it unusual as a prediction. Probably anyone who knew how the Jews throughout the empire had treated Paul in various cities could have "predicted" with no revelation from the Holy Spirit at all that Paul would meet violent opposition from the Jews in Jerusalem. What was unique about Agabus' prophecy was this prediction of "binding" and "delivering into the hands of the Gentiles." And on these two key elements, he is just a bit wrong.[230]

---

[229]Scott Cunningham, *"Through Many Tribulations": The Theology of Persecution in Luke-Acts* (Journal for the Study of the New Testament: Supplement Series 142; Sheffield: Sheffield Academic Press, 1997) 271.

[230]Grudem, *The Gift of Prophecy in the New Testament and Today*, 79. By "unusual," Grudem means that the details Agabus provides are unique in relation to previous revelation concerning Paul.

So then, Agabus cannot be seen as someone with negligible mistakes, but a prophet with major blunders. In the same breath, Grudem admits that the details of Paul's arrest are collectively "the heart of his prophecy" and what makes the prediction "unique," but he wants to minimize these as small errors. However, to say that Jews will bind Paul, when in reality no such event takes place, is no small error! Agabus is not merely "somewhat wrong" or "just a bit wrong." There is no redeeming Agabus once Grudem's arguments are accepted, since those details are essential to the prophet's utterance.

### Causative Fulfillment View

As an alternative to the general fulfillment view, some have taken a different position.[231] Though Jews do not actually bind and deliver Paul into the hands of the Gentiles, their belligerence causes Paul to be bound and delivered. Thus the Jews are ultimately responsible for Paul's imprisonment. Amongst the commentators and scholars that have committed to this view, Daniel Wallace explains the position in detail as he exposits the causative verb aspect. He writes concerning Acts 21:11:

> The prophecy by Agabus (already identified as a true prophet in Acts 11:28) was fulfilled in Acts 21:33 (where a Roman tribune arrested Paul and ordered him to be bound) and in the remainder of the book (where Paul is successively brought, as prisoner, up the chain of command until he got to Rome). Paul was not, strictly speaking, *bound* by the Jews, but by the Romans because a riot was breaking out

---

[231]The following scholars adhere to the causative fulfillment view based on different reasons: David B. McWilliams, "Something New Under the Sun?" *WTJ* 54:2 (1992) 325-26; Conzelmann, *The Acts of the Apostles*, 178; Cunningham, *"Through Many Tribulations,"* 271; Gentry, Jr., *The Charismatic Gift of Prophecy*, 43; Marshall, *The Acts of the Apostles*, 422; Thomas, "Prophecy Rediscovered?" 91; Williams, *Acts*, 362; Gaventa, *Acts*, 294-95; Bock, *Acts*, 638.

in the temple over Paul. And he was not, strictly speaking, *handed over* by the Jews to the Romans, but was in fact arrested and later protected by the Romans because of a Jewish plot to kill him. What are we to say of this prophecy? Only that because of Jews' *actions* Paul was bound and handed over to the Gentiles. They were the unwitting cause, but the cause nevertheless.[232]

*Examples of causative verbs*

Causative verbs are not novelties in the Koine Greek language. There are three notable instances in NT. The first instance involves Pilate and Jesus, with Roman soldiers as the intermediate party. Thomas points out John, who narrates that ἔλαβεν ὁ Πιλᾶτος τὸν Ἰησοῦν καὶ ἐμαστίγωσεν (Pilate took and scourged Jesus), though Pilate is not directly involved (John 19:1).[233]

Also, Peter later accuses the Jews of προσπήξαντες (nailing) Jesus when in fact Romans are the ones who carry out the act (Acts 2:23).[234] Paul also accuses the Jews of ἀποκτεινάντων Ἰησοῦν (killing Jesus) (1 Thess 2:14-15). In this instance, Jews and Christ are involved, with Roman soldiers as the intermediate party once again.

The third incident involves the fate of Judas, who betrays Jesus. Luke recounts that Judas ἐκτήσατο χωρίον (purchased a field), where his body lay (Acts 1:18). However, without doubt Judas returns the thirty pieces of silver to those who gave them to him and proceeds to commit suicide (Matt 27:3-5). The chief priests are the

---

[232]Daniel A. Wallace, *Greek Grammar Beyond the Basics: An Exegetical Syntax of the New Testament* (Grand Rapids: Zondervan, 1996) 412.

[233]Thomas, "Prophecy Rediscovered?," 91

[234]Ibid.; Oldham, "The Gift of Prophecy and Modern Revivals," 125; Gentry, Jr., *The Charismatic Gift of Prophecy,* 43; McWilliams, "Something New Under the Sun?" 326.

ones who purchase this field (Matt 27:7). So unless a causative fulfillment view is utilized here, Luke is blatantly wrong. Wallace explains:

> The text seems to suggest that Judas himself purchased the field in which he was later buried. However, Matt 27:7 specifically states that the *chief priests* purchased the field after Judas had died. It would be difficult to reconcile these two texts from the English point of view. But from the Greek, it is easy to see ἐκτήσατο as a *causative* middle, indicating that ultimately Judas purchased the field, in that it was purchased with his "blood money." Another possibility here is that since this verb never had an active form, it might be deponent, having the force of a causative *active.* However, it seems that it retains a middle *force* from classical to Koine Greek, and thus should be considered a true middle. In classical Greek (especially in Sophocles, Eurides, and Thucidydes) κτάομαι often had the causative nuance of "bring misfortune upon oneself" (cf. LSJ, BAGD). Such a nuance may even be appropriate in a secondary role to "acquire" in Acts 1:18.[235]

Besides the events surrounding the passion of Christ, Wallace lists other verses where the causative verb is found. For example, in Matthew 5:45, Jesus teaches that God τὸν ἥλιον αὐτοῦ ἀνατέλλει...καὶ βρέχει (causes His sun to rise...and causes it to rain).[236] In John 3:22, the apostle narrates that Jesus ἐβάπτιζεν (was baptizing), but

---

[235] Wallace, *Greek Grammar Beyond the Basics*, 424. See also John Murray, "Inspiration and Inerrancy," *Collected Writings of John Murray: Studies in Theology* (Edinburg: Banner of Truth, 1983) 4:28; and Gentry, Jr., *The Charismatic Gift of Prophecy,* 43.

[236] Wallace, *Greek Grammar Beyond the Basics*, 411.

in fact His disciples were performing the ritual (John 4:1-2). The causative nuance of this verb is revealed by the later verses.[237] God also causes the church to grow (ηὔξανεν) (1 Cor 3:6).[238] Wallace lists other instances to legitimize the case for the causative verb.[239]

Another important corollary of the causative fulfillment view is that a suitable explanation for the lack of volition in verbs is provided. Judas certainly does not actively intend to purchase the field, being dead already (Acts 1:18). This view further resolves the issue concerning volition in verbs.[240] Wallace writes:

> The cause may be *volitional*, but is not necessarily so. Volition is sometimes incorrectly assumed to be an essential part of a causative verb. Certainly it is one kind of source behind an action, but both personal and impersonal subjects act involuntarily at times and in such a way that they become unwitting sources of another action.[241]

However, a more critical observation of this view reveals some weaknesses. While in every example stated above save one (Acts 1:18) the causative nuance is clear or strongly implied, such is not the case with Acts 21:11. The samples of the causative above not only have a causative aspect, but a willing subject. For example, God is willing that the sun rises and the church grow (Matt

---

[237]Ibid., 412.

[238]Ibid.

[239]Ibid. Other instances include Acts 16:3; Gal 2:4; Eph 4:16; 1 Pet 1:22; Jude 13; Rev 7:15; 8;6. Furthermore, Greco-Roman literature also contains causative verbs. Herbert Smyth lists several examples from *Xenophenon*. Herbert W. Smyth, *Greek Grammar* (Cambridge: Harvard University, 1956) 390, 92.

[240]However, one does not need to take this causative fulfillment view to resolve the issue of volition in verbs. See discussion above.

[241]Ibid., 423.

5:45; 1 Cor 3:6). Jesus directs and causes His disciples to baptize (John 3:22; 4:1-2). Pilate orders Jesus to be scourged (John 19:1). The Jews demand that Jesus be crucified (John 19:15; Acts 2:23; 1 Thess 2:14-15). All of these subjects are actually willing and causing the action, not merely causing the action. Thus the only verse stated by Wallace that is truly analogous with Acts 21:11 is Acts 1:18. Judas is without will because he is dead when the field is purchased. With only a single verse for support, no sizable number of cases exists to substantiate the causative fulfillment view.

*Chronology of prophetic details.*

Another problem with the causative fulfillment view is chronology. This view does not adequately account for the order of events predicted by Agabus. In Acts 21:11, Agabus predicts that the Jews will bind Paul in Jerusalem and then deliver him into the hands of the Gentiles (δήσουσιν ἐν Ἰερουσαλὴμ οἱ Ἰουδαῖοι καὶ παραδώσουσιν εἰς χεῖρας ἐθνῶν). It appears that the binding process must take place first, regardless of whether Jews directly perform the act or cause the event to happen. Yet in Acts 21:33, Paul is delivered first and then chained. Luke narrates, τότε ἐγγίσας ὁ χιλίαρχος ἐπελάβετο αὐτοῦ καὶ ἐκέλευσε δεθῆναι ἁλύσεσι δυσί (Then the chiliarch approached and seized him and commanded him to be bound with two chains). Paul is already in Roman custody, "delivered" to the Gentile Romans from Jews, before he is bound. Acts 21:33 is certainly the point where the exchange occurs, but the "binding" must take place before. There is the problem of anachronism with this view. [242]

---

[242] One must consider the proper function of conjunction καὶ (and). The conjunction serves as a connective, adding an "element to a discussion" or an "idea to the train of thought." So then, the conjunction itself does not necessarily imply chronological order without additional clues such as "first" or "then," as in Romans 1:16.

*Assumed Fulfillment View*

The last view maintains that Paul is bound by the Jews and delivered to the Gentiles even though Luke does not explicitly report all of the details in his narrative. In this scheme, the transfer of custody takes place in Acts 21:33 and the binding is assumed to take place before the chiliarch arrives.

Some scholars have adopted this view. William J. Larkin writes: "Though neither of these actions is recorded, both are assumed in what Luke tells us of the Jews' treatment and the Romans' handling of Paul (21:30-33; 24:1-9; compare 28:17). We do not need to conclude, as many do, that based on Luke's report of the arrest, Agabus is mistaken."[243] Homer A. Kent Jr. is also helpful here as he offers a solution:

> The details of the prophecy would lead one to expect something slightly different from what eventually happened. In the prophecy the Jews would bind Paul (but in 21:33 it was the Romans who did it), and would deliver him to the gentiles (actually, the Romans took Paul away from the Jews). However, the main point is clear that Paul would be seized by the Jews and then fall into the hands of the gentiles. It is not inconceivable, however, that the Jews did bind him first (21:30), and their delivering of him to the Romans could be understood as forced rather than voluntary.[244]

This assumption view is not far-fetched when Acts 28:17 is considered. Paul recounts the Jerusalem scene in

---

However, this problem cannot be dismissed, because it is illogical for Jews to bind Paul after they have transferred him. Wallace, *Greek Grammar Beyond the Basics*, 671.

[243] Larkin Jr., *Acts*, 304.

[244] Homer A. Kent Jr., *Jerusalem to Rome: Studies in the Book of Acts* (Grand Rapids: Baker, 1972) 160 footnote 27.

that verse, stating, δέσμιος ἐξ Ἱεροσολύμων παρεδόθην εἰς τὰς χεῖρας τῶν Ῥωμαίων (I was delivered as a prisoner from Jerusalem into the hands of the Romans). Two observations are in order. First, Paul recalls the events in Jerusalem when he is ambushed by the Jewish mob and given over to the Roman soldiers. Secondly and most importantly, Paul considers himself a "prisoner" (de,smioj), even before he is placed in chains. One can safely assume that a prisoner is bound. So then, the assumed fulfillment prophecy view is not implausible.

### Examples of assumed fulfillment

In both OT and NT, there are examples of prophecy of events assumed to have taken place in the subsequent narrative. For example, in the OT, Rechabites are guaranteed future existence for their adherence to their tradition, but this is assumed to be fulfilled without any explicit remarks from Jeremiah (Jer 35:19). In the NT, Nathanael is promised a vision of opened heavens, transporting angels, and the Son of Man (John 1:51). However, there is no explicit confirmation from John that this prophecy is fulfilled.

### Lukan narratives of arrests

Accordingly, Luke's narrative style allows for this assumption view. Luke may have left out a detail from the frantic arrest scene in the temple. He certainly leaves out a detail in Jesus' arrest. When one compares the four accounts of the gospel writers describing the moment of Jesus' arrest in Gethsemane, one discovers that Luke does not mention the binding process even though it is clear that Jesus is bound. In Matthew 26:57, Matthew uses the word κρατήσαντες (from κρατέω, seize) to describe the incident. In Mark 14:46, Mark adds that they ἐπέβαλαν τὰς χεῖρας (laid their hands) on them. Luke uses a different word, Συλλαβόντες (from συλλαμβάνω, arrest), to describe the incident (Luke 22:54). From the accounts of the synoptic gospel writers alone, it appears that Jesus is simply seized by the hands of the mob.

However, John narrates that the mob συνέλαβον τὸν Ἰησοῦν καὶ ἔδησαν αὐτὸν (arrested Jesus and bound him) (John 18:12). John uses the same word that Luke uses to describe the arrest (συλλαμβάνω), but adds that Jesus is bound. Perhaps Luke considered the verb συλλαμβάνω (arrest) an adequate expression wherein the binding is assumed. His readers can logically infer that Jesus is bound at Gethsemane. Such inference is not beyond reason if the readers understand that the procedures for an arrest would necessitate a binding process.

The same case applies to Paul when he is in the midst of the Jewish mob. Claudius Lysias recounts the mob scene and uses the same word συλλαμβάνω (arrest) used by Luke and John to describe the arrest of Jesus (Luke 22:54; John 18:12; Acts 23:27). Note the bold, italicized, and underlined words on the table below. The commander writes in his official letter that τὸν ἄνδρα τοῦτον συλλημφθέντα ὑπὸ τῶν Ἰουδαίων (this man was arrested by the Jews). It is likely that Luke considers this word συλλαμβάνω (arrest) as an adequate expression to describe the entire process which includes seizing with hands, restraining with force, and binding with ropes.

So then, it is not difficult to imagine that sometime during the frenzied scene, Paul is bound by the Jews (Acts 21:27-32). As Kent proposes, the binding could have taken place in Acts 21:30, when the crowd ἐπιλαβόμενοι τοῦ Παύλου (took hold of Paul).[245] Or the binding could have taken place earlier in Acts 21:27 when the Jews from Asia stirred up the crowd and together ἐπέβαλον ἐπ' αὐτὸν τὰς χεῖρας (laid their hands upon him). Note on the table below how this passage shares

---

[245]Kent Jr., *Jerusalem to Rome*, 160 footnote 27.

the bold and italicized words with Mark 14:46). Either way, it is not unreasonable to assume that a mob would bind their victim before inflicting damage. The synoptic gospel writers had no qualms about making such assumptions.

|  | Jesus at Gethsemane | Paul in Jerusalem Temple |
|---|---|---|
| Matthew 26:57 | κρατήσαντες (from κρατέω, seize) |  |
| Mark 14:46 | *ἐπέβαλαν τὰς χεῖρας* (*laid their hands*) |  |
| Luke 22:54 | <u>**Συλλαβόντες**</u> (from συλλαμβάνω, <u>*arrest*</u>) |  |
| John 18:12 | <u>**συνέλαβον**</u> τὸν Ἰησοῦν καὶ ἔδησαν αὐτὸν (<u>*arrested*</u> Jesus and bound him) |  |
| Acts 21:27 |  | *ἐπέβαλον* ἐπ' αὐτὸν *τὰς χεῖρας* (*laid their hands* upon him) |
| Acts 21:30 |  | ἐπιλαβόμενοι τοῦ Παύλου |

| | | |
|---|---|---|
| | | (took hold of Paul) |
| Acts 23:27 | | τὸν ἄνδρα τοῦτον **_συλλημφθέντα_** ὑπὸ τῶν Ἰουδαίων (this man was <u>*arrested*</u> by the Jews) |

*Preferred View*

Among the three views the preferred view must be sought. Grudem is too bold to say that Luke contradicts the details of Agabus' prophecy.[246] There are three reasons to reject the general fulfillment view. First, a firm belief in inspiration and inerrancy precludes notions of mistakes in Agabus' prophecy. Secondly, actual verbal correspondence exists once Acts 28:17 is compared with Acts 21:11. Thirdly, since the details are essentially the prophecy of Agabus itself, either Agabus is completely wrong or completely correct. There is no place for semi-accurate prophecy. The general fulfillment view cannot prevail.

The causative fulfillment view is opposed to the view of Grudem. The unchecked violence of the Jewish mob causes Paul to be delivered and bound by the Roman soldiers. However, there is very little support for a causative verb that lacks will in the part of the subject. Only Acts 1:18 can support this view. The causative fulfillment view is unfounded.

For these reasons, the assumed fulfillment view is the preferred view. Though Luke does not overtly

---

[246]Grudem, *The Gift of Prophecy in the New Testament and Today*, 80.

confirm Agabus' prophecy in his narrative, one can be confident that the prophet utters a genuine revelation that is fulfilled. It is an acceptable practice of biblical writers to record prophecies without their subsequent fulfillment, or without describing every detail in the fulfillment, as is the case with this imprisonment prophecy. Luke uses συλλαμβάνω (arrest) to summarize the entire process where Jews grab, restrain, and tie up Paul. Readers can reasonably infer from Acts 21 that Jews bind Paul and hand him over.

### Conclusion

This chapter dealt with the nature of the imprisonment prophecy and its fulfillment. Acts 21:10-11 is a NT prophecy that predicts Paul's arrest in Jerusalem. The nature of Agabus' prophecy is largely revealed in the studies of the prophetic act, the citation (τάδε λέγει τὸ πνεῦμα τὸ ἅγιον (Thus says the Holy Spirit), the binding, and the transfer. Paul is to be bound physically by Jews and delivered to the Gentiles.

The fulfillment of this prophecy can be explained in at least three ways. One can generally confirm its fulfillment without affirming the details. Another view is that the Jews cause the Romans to fulfill the prophecy. Still another view is that the prophecy is fulfilled, albeit there is no explicit account of fulfillment. This last view prevails over others.

# CHAPTER V

# CONCLUSION

The purpose of this study has been to evaluate the accuracy of Agabus' prophecy. The study of Agabus' prophecy is occasioned by several factors. The ongoing debate between the cessationists and the non-cessationists bolstered by recent scholastic interest in biblical prophecy provides the setting for this study. The neglect of content-focused study of prophecy also motivates this research into Agabus' prophecies. Within the bounds of certain commonly-held convictions such as the inspiration and the inerrancy of Scriptures and the historicity of Acts, this study has focused on investigating whether Agabus' prophecies are characterized by foretelling accuracy. The method used has been exegetical evaluation of the nature of prophecies recorded in Acts and the available sources that confirm them. The following sections will provide a summary of research and some important implications for the modern church.

## Summary of the Preceding Discussion

From chapters II to IV, various positions concerning the foretelling accuracy of Agabus have been presented, with evaluations of Agabus' famine prophecy and imprisonment prophecy. In chapter II, the two main views concerning Agabus' prophecies were studied. On one hand, some scholars have adopted the view of Wayne Grudem, which is called fallible NT prophecy view. Within the utterances of NT prophets are elements that are either from man—therefore erroneous or from God—therefore true. In this view, apostles, not the NT prophets, are the true heirs of OT prophets and equal in status. Grudem gathers much of his support from 1 Corinthians. Since Agabus is wrong in details of his two prophecies, hearers must sift between the human elements and the divine revelation. Influential scholars such D. A. Carson, Graham Houston, Max Turner, and Sam Storms have adopted the view of Grudem with slight modifications.

On the other hand, are scholars who adhere to the infallible NT prophecy view. This is the traditional view that asserts the inspiration and the inerrancy of the NT prophetic message. Two representatives, Richard Gaffin and F. David Farnell, establish the connection between the OT prophet, the apostle, and the NT prophet. Consequently, Agabus proclaims prophecy that is on par with the authority of Scriptures, containing no mistakes.

In chapter III, Agabus' famine prophecy in Acts 11:28 was studied. The prophecy pertains to the Roman Empire, is delivered in cogent, predictive speech, and sourced in the Holy Spirit without a hint of human influence. Luke confirms the fulfillment of the famine prophecy in the very verse he describes the prediction (Acts 11:28). Supplemental support comes from various secular sources. According to Kenneth Gapp, the different episodes of famines during the reign of Claudius are bound together through the Roman Empire's dependence on Egyptian imports. A universal famine does not correlate with universal hunger, but with the intensification of hunger among the poorer classes in the society.

In chapter IV, Agabus' imprisonment prophecy in Acts 21:10-11 was studied. This prophecy pertains to Paul's fate in Jerusalem. The combination of the prophetic act and the speech which ensues indicate that Paul will be physically bound, with the Jews as the culprits, and then delivered over to the Gentiles. The

Holy Spirit is cited as the ultimate source of this prophecy.

There are at least three views concerning the fulfillment of this prophecy. One view concludes that Agabus is generally correct in his prophecy, but that he errs in the details. However, since those details compose the essential portion of the prophecy, any error therein would be critical. Another camp holds that the fervor of the Jewish mob in Jerusalem causes Paul to be bound and delivered over to the Romans. However, there is little support for a verb with a volition-less subject. Anachronism is also a problem. The last view is the assumed fulfillment view. This view holds that Paul is bound during the frantic mob scene before he is transferred, even though Luke does not explicitly state such a detail. The binding can be reasonably and necessarily assumed in the narrative account of Acts, based on the proper understanding of δέσμιος (prisoner) and συλλαμβάνω (arrest). Since such assumption of fulfillment is common in the Bible, one does not need to doubt the fulfillment of the imprisonment prophecy in its details.

## Implications for the Modern Church

Based on the conclusions of this study, the modern church is driven to a renewed assessment of NT prophecy and the overarching Pneumatology. Two subjects are in order. The growing number of charismatic and Pentecostal believers, combined with Grudem's widespread influence, requires evaluation of the modern church. A study of church history is also necessary. Since the recent controversies are occupied in the context of church history, and not in a time vacuum, similar controversies in history must be studied. The Montanist crisis in the early church immediately comes to mind. Both implications will be briefly discussed.

*Growing non-cessationism and Grudem*

Generally speaking, there is a widespread diversity among churches concerning spiritual gifts today. In the new millennium, the basic idea of non-cessationism survives. Spontaneous gifts of tongues, healing, and prophecy from Pentecostal roots are claimed worldwide, among the Indian Catholics, Ethiopian Lutherans, Singapore Baptists, Korean Presbyterians, South American Moravians, South African Zionists, and indigenous Christians in China.[247] Jenkins reports in 2007 that about one out of every five evangelical Christians in the world is neither Protestant, Orthodox, or Anglican, but is an "Independent," a category dominated by Pentecostal distinctives.[248] The numerical majority of Christianity is shifting to the followers of Pentecostal/charismatic teachings. The traditional view of cessationism is not held by the many of the newer churches today.

Concerning the gift of prophecy, the growing number of non-cessationists has the support of a scholastic voice in Grudem now. With the endorsement of such a prominent scholar, the growing number of charismatics who claim to have prophetic phenomena at their respective churches have a major champion for their practices.[249] Since Grudem is considered conservative in theology, no longer can non-charismatics such as David J. Hesselgrave freely accuse the charismatics of being

---

[247] Gary B. McGee, "Surprises of the Holy Spirit: How Pentecostalism Has Changed the Landscape of Modern Mission," *Between Past and Future: Evangelical Mission Entering the Twenty-First Century* (Evangelical Missionary Society Series; ed. Jonathan J. Bonk; Pasadena, CA: William Carey Library, 2003) 62.

[248] Jenkins, *The Next Christendom*, 70.

[249] Grudem does urge that certain guidelines govern the practice of the gift. For example, one should not introduce their "prophecies" with words such as "thus say the Lord" or speak in the first person for God. Grudem, *The Gift of Prophecy in the New Testament and Today*, 225-26.

"doctrineless."[250] It is inevitable that cessationists must interact with Grudem's ideas.[251]

*Parallels to previous church controversies*

While discussion in this paper concerns exegesis of key passages in a content-based study of NT prophecy, there is much room for exploration of historical issues. Grudem avers that many Puritans, such as Samuel Rutherford and Richard Baxter, support his view.[252] He also cites the Westminster Confession of Faith as a supporting document.[253] Other scholars arrive at similar conclusions, based on studies of earlier texts such as the *Shepherd of Hermas*.[254]

---

[250]David J. Hesselgrave, *Today's Choices for Tomorrow's Mission: An Evangelical Perspective on Trends and Issues in Missions* (Grand Rapids, MI: Academie Books, 1988) 128.

[251]Another prominent scholar who endorses views of prophecy similar to Grudem is Cecil M. Robeck Jr. He writes in some familiar words: "To guarantee that the prophetic offerings were indeed the mind of the Holy Spirit, Paul noted that an assessment needed to be made. It was an assessment of *what was spoken* (content) more than it was an assessment of *the person who spoke* (medium). In his instructions written to the Thessalonian Christians, Paul had already exhorted the church not to quench the Spirit or to despise prophesying. Instead he had offered the advice to *test* it (*dokimazete*), accepting what was good in it while avoiding what was not (1 Thess. 5:19-22)." Cecil M. Robeck, Jr., "Gift of Prophecy," *The New International Pentecostal Dictionary of Pentecostal and Charismatic Movements* (eds. Stanley M. Burgess and Eduard M. van der Maas; Revised and Expanded ed; Grand Rapids: Zondervan, 2002) 1004.

[252]Grudem, *The Gift of Prophecy in the New Testament and Today*, 13.

[253]Grudem writes, "...the *Westminster Confession of Faith* apparently referred to such private informative revelations from the Holy Spirit as 'private spirits' and counted them along with 'opinions of ancient writers' and 'doctrines of men' as things that exist in the church but that are to be judged by 'the Holy Spirit speaking in the Scripture' (WCF 1:10)—a view with which I would heartily agree." Ibid., 13-14.

[254]Jannes Reiling, "Prophecy, the Spirit and the Church," *Prophetic Vocation in the New Testament and Today* (ed. J.

Efforts to counter Grudem are leading scholars to reexamine historical figures and documents. For example, Gentry cites the third section of "The Form of Government" from the original Westminster Assembly to support the idea of cessation.[255] Farnell gathers lessons from the Montanist controversy.[256] Farnell maintains that no middle ground or mixture of human and divine was tolerated during the resolution of this controversy.[257] The debate between cessationists and non-cessationists continues in the new arena of historical theology.

*Conclusion*

Agabus' legacy is defined in the two prophecies recorded in Acts 11:28 and 21:10-11. Nothing in the immediate context of those verses suggests that Grudem's view of prophecy can be supported. Though not much is known concerning Agabus, his contribution to the Antiochene congregation, the poor believers of Jerusalem, the Caesarean congregation, and especially the Apostle Paul should not be undermined. NT prophetic gift was a vital part of the early church that edifies, exhorts, and consoles (1 Cor 14:3).

Furthermore, the study of Agabus' prophecy leads one to conclude that NT prophecy is divine revelation that should not be doubted. Human mistakes are not included in the manifestation of this gift. The Holy Spirit is not only the source of the divine revelation but the

---

Panagopoulos; Supplement to Novum Testamentum, Vol XLV; Leiden: E. J. Brill, 1977) 71-76.

[255] Gentry, *The Charismatic Gift of Prophecy*, 121-22.

[256] Carson asserts that this controversy demands special attention, since Montanists' demise marked the end of major prophetic claims until the 20th century. Carson, *Showing the Spirit*, 166.

[257] Thomas, "Prophesy Rediscovered?" 96; For a full discussion, see F. David Farnell, "The Montanist Crisis: A Key to Refuting Third-wave Concepts of NT Prophecy," *Master's Seminary Journal* (2003) 235-262.

One who guarantees safe transmission of the message to the congregation.

# BIBLIOGRAPHY

*The Apostolic Fathers.* Trans. by J. B. Lightfoot and J. R. Harmer. Edited and Revised by Michael W. Holmes. Second Edition. Grand Rapids: Baker, 1989.

Aune, David E. *Prophecy in Early Christian and the Ancient Mediterranean World.* Grand Rapids: Eerdmans, 1983.

Balz, Horst and Gerhard Schneider eds. *Exegetical Dictionary of the New Testament.* 3 vols. Grand Rapids, MI: Eerdmans, 1990.

Barret, C. K. *A Critical and Exegetical Commentary on the Acts of the Apostles.* International Critical Commentary. 2 vols. Edinburgh: T&T Clark, 1994.

Bauer, W., F. W. Danker, W. Arndt, and F. W. Gingrich. *A Greek-English Lexicon of the New Testament and Other Early Christian Literature.* Third Edition. Chicago, IL: The University of Chicago Press, 2000.

Bauer, W., W. Arndt, F. W. Gingrich, and F. W. Danker. *A Greek-English Lexicon of the New Testament and Other Early Christian Literature.* Second Edition. Chicago, IL: The University of Chicago Press, 1979.

Boak, Arthur E. R. *Papyri from Tebtunis, Part I.* Michigan Papyri, Vol. II. Ann Arbor: University of Michigan Press, 1933.

Bock, Darrell L. *Acts.* Baker Exegetical Commentary on the New Testament. Grand Rapids: Baker Academic, 2007.

Bruce, F. F. *The Book of Acts.* New International Commentary on the New Testament. Grand Rapids: Eerdmans, 1988.

_____. *The Acts of the Apostles: Greek Text with Introduction and Commentary.* Grand Rapids: Eerdmans, 1990.

Burgess, Stanley M. and Eduard M. van der Maas. *The New International Pentecostal Dictionary of Pentecostal and Charismatic Movements.* Revised and Expanded Edition. Grand Rapids: Zondervan, 2002.

Caird, George B. *The Language and Imagery of the Bible.* Philadelphia: Westminster, 1980.

Calvin, John. *The Acts of the Apostles: Chapters 14-28.* Trans. John W. Fraser. Ed. David W. Torrance and Thomas F. Torrance. Grand Rapids: Eerdmans, 1966.

Carson, D. A. *Showing the Spirit: A Theological Exposition of 1 Corinthians 12-14.* Grand Rapids: Baker, 1987.

Cary, Ernest and Herbert B. Foster, trans. *Dio Cassius.* Loeb Classical Library. 9 vols. Cambridge: Harvard University Press, 1914-27.

Conzelmann, Hans. *The Acts of the Apostles.* Hermeneia. Philadelphia: Fortress, 1987.

*Corpus Inscriptionum Graecarum.* Ed. A. Boeckh. 4 Vols. Berlin: Ex Officina Academica, 1828-77.

Cosgrave, Charles H. "The Divine Dei in Luke-Acts: Investigations into the Lukan Understanding of God's Providence." *Novum Testamentum 26* (1984) 168-90.

Culy, Martin M. and Mikeal C. Parsons. *Acts: A Handbook on the Greek Text.* Waco: Baylor University Press, 2003.

Cunningham, Scott. *"Through Many Tribulations": The Theology of Persecution in Luke-Acts.* Journal for the Study of the New Testament: Supplement Series 142. Sheffield: Sheffield Academic Press, 1997.

Deferrari, Roy J., trans. *Paulus Orosius: The Seven Books of History Against the Pagans.* Washington: Catholic University of America Press, 1964.

De Zwaan, J. "The Use of the Greek Language in Acts." *Beginnings of Christianity: Part I: The Acts of the Apostles.* Ed. F. J. Foakes Jackson and Kirsopp Lake. 5 vols. Grand Rapids: Baker, 1979.

Edgar, Thomas R. *Miraculous Gifts: Are They for Today?* Neptune, NJ: Loizeaux Brothers, 1983.

_____. *Satisfied by the Promise of the Spirit.* Grand Rapids: Kregel, 1996.

Ellis, E. Earle. "Prophecy in the New Testament Church—and Today." *Prophetic Vocation in the New Testament and Today.* Ed. J. Panagopoulos. Supplement to Novum Testamentum, Vol XLV. Leiden: E. J. Brill, 1977.

"Evangelical Leader Leaves Wife for Man." *Christianity Today* 43 (November 15, 1999) 29.

Farnell, F. David. "The Montanist Crisis: A Key to Refuting Third-wave Concepts of NT Prophecy." *Master's Seminary Journal* (2003) 235-262.

_____. "The New Testament Prophetic Gift: Its Nature and Duration." Ph.D. dissertation, Dallas Theological Seminary, Dallas, Texas, 1990.

_____. "Fallible New Testament Prophecy/Prophets? A Critique of Wayne Grudem's Hypothesis." *The Master's Seminary Journal* 2 (1991) 157-80.

_____. "Is the Gift of Prophecy for Today? Part 1: The Current Debate about New Testament Prophecy." *Bibliotheca Sacra* 149 (1992) 277-303.

_____. "Is the Gift of Prophecy for Today? Part 2: The Gift of Prophecy in the Old and New Testaments." *Bibliotheca Sacra* 149 (1992) 387-410.

_____. "Is the Gift of Prophecy for Today? Part 3: Does the New Testament Teach Two Prophetic Gifts?" *Bibliotheca Sacra* 150 (1993) 62-88.

_____. "Is the Gift of Prophecy for Today? Part 4: When Will the Gift of Prophecy Cease?" *Bibliotheca Sacra* 150 (1993) 171-202.

Fernando, Aijith. *Acts.* NIV Application Commentary. Grand Rapids: Zondervan, 1998.

Fitzmeyer, Jospeph A. *The Acts of the Apostles: A New Translation with Introduction and Commentary.* Anchor Bible 31. New York: Doubleday, 1998.

Foakes-Jackson, F. J. *The Acts of the Apostles.* Moffatt New Testament Commentary. London: Hodder & Stoughton, 1951.

Gaebelein, A. C. *The Acts of the Apostles: An Exposition.* New York: Our Hope, 1912.

Gaffin Jr., Richard B. "Prophecy and Tongues." *Perspectives on Pentecost.* Phillipsburg, NJ: Presbyterian and Reformed, 1979.

_____. "A Cessationist View." *Are Miraculous Gifts for Today? Four Views.* Counterpoints. Ed. Wayne A. Grudem. Grand Rapids, MI: Zondervan, 1996.

Gapp, Kenneth S. "The Universal Famine under Claudius." *Harvard Theological Review* 28:4 (1935) 258-265.

Gasque, W. W. *A History of the Interpretation of the Acts of the Apostles.* Peabody, MA: Hendrickson, 1989.

Gaventa, B. R. *Acts.* Abingdon New Testament Commentaries. Nashville: Abingdon, 2003.

Gentry Jr., Kenneth L. *The Charismatic Gift of Prophecy: A Reformed Response to Wayne Grudem.* Eugene, OR: Wipf & Stock, 2000.

Green, Michael. *I Believe in the Holy Spirit.* Grand Rapids: Eerdmans, 1975.

Grudem, Wayne A. *The Gift of Prophecy in 1 Corinthians.* Washington: University, 1982.

_____. *The Gift of Prophecy in the New Testament and Today.* Revised Edition. Westchester, IL: Crossway Books, 2000.

_____. *Systematic Theology.* Grand Rapids: Zondervan, 1994.

_____. "Preface." *Are Miraculous Gifts for Today? Four Views.* Counterpoints. Ed. Wayne A. Grudem. Grand Rapids, MI: Zondervan, 1996.

Haenchen, Ernst. *The Acts of the Apostles: A Commentary.* Trans. by Bernard Noble and Gerald Shinn. Oxford: Blackwell, 1987.

Harmon, A. M., et al., trans. *Lucian.* Loeb Classical Library. 8 vols. Cambridge: Harvard University Press, 1913-67.

Harrison, E. F. *Acts: The Expanding Church.* Chicago: Moody, 1975.

Hengel, Martin. *Acts and the History of the Earliest Christianity.* Philadelphia: Fortress Press 1979.

Hesselgrave, David J. *Today's Choices for Tomorrow's Mission: An Evangelical Perspective on Trends and Issues in Missions.* Grand Rapids, MI: Academie Books, 1988.

Hilber, John W. "Diversity of OT Prophetic Phenomena and NT Prophecy." *Westminster Theological Journal* 56 (1994) 243-258.

Hill, David. *New Testament Prophecy.* New Foundations Theological Library. Atlanta: John Knox Press, 1979.

Houghton, Myron J. "A Reexamination of 1 Corinthians 13:8-13." *Bibilotheca Sacra* 153 (1996) 344-56.

Houston, Graham. *Prophecy: A Gift for Today?* Downers Grove, IL: InterVarsity Press, 1989.

Hutton, M., et al., trans. *Tacitus.* Loeb Classical Library. 5 vols. Cambridge: Harvard University Press, 1914-37.

Jenkins, Philip. *The Next Christendom: The Coming of Global Christianity.* New York, NY: Oxford, 2007.

Jeremias, Joachim. "Sabbathjahr und neutestamentliche Chronologie." Zeitschrift für die Neutestamentliche Wissenschaft und Kunde der Älteren Kirche (1928) 98-103.

Jervell J. *The Theology of the Acts of the Apostles.* New Testament Theology. Cambridge: Cambridge University Press, 1996.

Johnson, Luke Timothy. *The Acts of the Apostles.* Sacra Pagina 5. Collegeville, MN: The Liturgical Press, 1991.

Keener, Craig S. *Acts: An Exegetical Commentary.* 4 vols. Grand Rapids: Baker Academic: 2012-15.

Kent Jr., Homer A. *Jerusalem to Rome: Studies in the Book of Acts.* Grand Rapids: Baker, 1972.

Kistemaker, Simon J. *Acts.* New Testament Commentary. Grand Rapids: Baker, 1990.

Kittel, G., and G. Friedrich, eds. *Theological Dictionary of the New Testament.* 10 vols. Grand Rapids, MI: Eerdmans, 1964-1976.

Lake, Kirsopp. "The Chronology of Acts." *Beginnings of Christianity: Part I: The Acts of the Apostles.* Ed. F. J. Foakes Jackson and Kirsopp Lake. 5 vols. Grand Rapids: Baker, 1979.

Lake, Kirsopp and J. E. L. Oulton, trans. *Eusebius.* Loeb Classical Library. 2 vols. Cambridge: Harvard University Press, 1926-32.

Larkin Jr., William J. *Acts.* IVP New Testament Commentary 5. Downer's Grove, IL: InterVarsity, 1995.

Lenski, R. C. H. *The Interpretation of the Acts of the Apostles.* Minneapolis: Augsburg Publishing House, 1934.

Liddell, H. G., and R. Scott. *A Greek-English Lexicon.* Oxford: Clarendon Press, 1990.

Longenecker, Richard N. "The Acts of the Apostles." *Expositor's Bible Commentary.* Ed.

F. Gaebelein. 12 vols. Grand Rapids: Zondervan, 1981.

Maddox, R. *The Purpose of Luke-Acts.* Forchungen zur Religion und Literatur des Alten und Neuen Testaments 127. Gottingen: Vandenhoeck & Ruprescht, 1982.

Marguerat, D. *The First Christian Historian: Writing the "Acts of the Apostles."* Trans. by K. McKinney, G. J. Laughery, and R. Bauckham. Society for New Testament Studies Monograph Series 121. Cambridge: Cambridge University Press, 2002.

Marshall, I. Howard. *The Acts of the Apostles: An Introduction and Commentary.* Tyndale New Testament Commentaries 5. Grand Rapids: Eerdmans, 1980.

_____. "Acts and the 'Former Treatise.'" *The Book of Acts in Its Ancient Literary Setting.* Ed. Bruce W. Winter and Andrew D. Clarke. The Book of Acts in Its First Century Setting 1. Grand Rapids: Eerdmans, 1993.

Maudlin, Michael G. "Seers in the Heartland." *Christianity Today* 35 (January 14, 1991) 18-22.

McGee, Gary B. "Surprises of the Holy Spirit: How Pentecostalism Has Changed the Landscape of Modern Mission." *Between Past and Future: Evangelical Mission Entering the Twenty-First Century.* Evangelical Missionary Society Series. Ed. Jonathan J. Bonk. Pasadena, CA: William Carey Library, 2003.

McWilliams, David B. "Something New Under the Sun?" *Westminster Theological Journal* 54:2 (1992) 321-330.

Metzger, Bruce M. The Canon of the New Testament: Its Origin, Development, and Significance. Oxford: Clarendon Press, 1997.

Moulton, James H., and George Milligan. The Vocabulary of the Greek Testament: Illustsrated from the Papyri and Other Non-Literary Sources. Grand Rapids, MI: Eerdmans, 1930.

Moulton, J. H., and N. Turner. *A Grammar of New Testament Greek.* 4 vols. Edinburgh: T&T Clark, 1963-76.

Munck, Johannes. *The Acts of the Apostles.* The Anchor Bible. Garden City, NY: Doubleday, 1967.

Murray, John. *Collected Writings of John Murray.* 4 vols. Edinburg: Banner of Truth, 1983.

Oldfather, W. A., trans. *Epictetus.* Loeb Classical Library. 2 vols. Cambridge: Harvard University Press, 1925-28.

Oldham, David. "The Gift of Prophecy and Modern Revivals." *Reformation and Revival* 5:1 (1996) 111-39.

Orosius, Paulus. *Pavli Orosii Historiarvm adversum paganos libri VII / ex recognitione Caroli Zangemeister.* Bibliotheca Scriptorum Graecorum et Romanorum Teubneriana. Lipsiae : in aedibvs B. G. Tevbneri, 1889.

Pearse, Roger., trans. *Chronicles of St. Jerome.* No pages. Cited 14 January 2010. Online:

http://www.tertullian.org/fathers/jerome_chronicle_03_part2.htm.

_____. *Chronicles of St. Jerome.* No pages. Cited 14 January 2010. Online:

http://www.ccel.org/ccel/pearse/morefathers/files/jerome_chronicle_06_latin_part2.htm.

Perrin, Bernadotte, et al., trans. *Plutarch.* Loeb Classical Library. 26 vols. Cambridge: Harvard University Press, 1910-2004.

Pervo, R. I. *Profit with Delight: The Literary Genre of the Acts of the Apostles.* Philadelphia: Fortress, 1987.

Pfeiffer, Charles F. *Between the Testaments.* Grand Rapids: Baker, 1959.

Polhill, J. B. *Acts.* New American Commentary 26. Nashville: Broadman, 1992.

Rackham H., et al., trans. *Pliny.* Loeb Classical Library. 10 vols. Cambridge: Harvard University Press, 1938-62.

Rackham, R. B. *The Acts of the Apostles: An Exposition.* Westminster Commentaries. London: Methuen, 1901.

Radl, W. *Paulus und Jesus im lukanischen Doppelwerk: Untersuchungen zu Parallelmotiven im*

Lukasevangelium und in der Apostelgeschichte. Bern: H. Lang/Frankfurt: P. Lang, 1975.

Ramsay, William M. *St. Paul: The Traveler and Roman Citizen.* Revised and Updated by Mark Wilson. Grand Rapids: Kregel, 2001.

Reiling, Jannes. "Prophecy, the Spirit and the Church." *Prophetic Vocation in the New Testament and Today.* Ed. J. Panagopoulos. Supplement to Novum Testamentum, Vol XLV. Leiden: E. J. Brill, 1977.

Riesner, Rainer. *Paul's Early Period: Chronology, Mission Strategy, Theology.* Trans. by Doug Stott. Grand Rapids: Eerdmans, 1998.

Robertson, A. T. *The Acts of the Apostles.* Word Pictures in the New Testament. 6 vols. Nashville: Broadman, 1930.

_____. *John/Hebrews.* Word Pictures in the New Testament. 6 vols. Nashville: Broadman, 1930.

_____. *A Grammar of the Greek New Testament in the Light of Historical Research.* Nashville: Broadman, 1934.

Rolfe, J. C., trans. *Suetonius.* Loeb Classical Library. 2 vols. Cambridge: Harvard University Press, 1914.

Rosner, Brian S. "Acts and Biblical History." *The Book of Acts in Its Ancient Literary Setting.* Ed. Bruce W. Winter and Andrew D. Clarke. The Book of Acts in Its First Century Setting 1. Grand Rapids: Eerdmans, 1993.

Sharp, Granville. *Remarks on the Uses of the Definite Article in the Greek Text of the New Testament: Containing Many New Proofs of the Divinity of Christ, from Passages which are wrongly Translated in the Common English Version.* 1st American ed. From the 3rd London ed. Philadelphia: Hopkins, 1807.

Smith, Charles F., trans. *Thucydides*. Loeb Classical Library. 4 vols. Cambridge: Harvard University Press, 1910-23.

Smyth, Herbert W. *Greek Grammar*. Cambridge: Harvard University, 1956.

Storms, Sam. *Practicing the Power: Welcoming the Gifts of the Holy Spirit in Your Life*. Grand Rapids: Zondervan, 2017.

Swanson, Dennis M. "Bibliography of Works on Cessationism." *Master's Seminary Journal* 14 (2003) 311-27.

Tenney, Merrill C. "The Influence of Antioch on Apostolic Christianity." *Bibliotheca Sacra* 107 (1950) 298-310.

Thackeray, Henry St. J., et al., trans. *Josephus*. Loeb Classical Library. 13 vols. Cambridge: Harvard University Press, 1926-65.

Thomas, Robert L. *Understanding Spiritual Gifts: The Christian's Special Gifts in the Light of 1 Corinthians 12-14*. Chicago: Moody Press, 1978.

_____. "Prophecy Rediscovered? Review of The Gift of Prophecy in the New Testament and Today." *Bibliotheca Sacra* 149 (1992) 83-96.

Torrey, Charles C. *The Composition and the Date of Acts*. Cambridge: Harvard University Press, 1916.

Toussaint, Stanley D. "Acts." *The Bible Knowledge Commentary 2*. Ed. John Walvoord and Roy Zuck. Colorado Springs, CO: Chariot Victor Publishing, 1983.

Turner, Max. "Spirit Endowment In Luke/Acts: Some Linguistic Considerations." *Vox Evangelica* 12 (1981) 45-63.

_____. "Spiritual Gifts Then and Now." *Vox Evangelica* 15 (1985) 7-63.

Turner, Nigel. *Grammatical Insights into the New Testament.* Edinburgh: T. & T. Clark, 1965.

Wagner, C. Peter. *Your Spiritual Gifts Can Help Your Church Grow.* Glendale: G/L Regal Books, 1976.

Wallace, Daniel A. "The Article-Noun-*kai*-Noun Plural Construction." *Grace Theological Journal* 4:1 (1983) 59-84.

_____. *Greek Grammar Beyond the Basics: An Exegetical Syntax of the New Testament.* Grand Rapids: Zondervan, 1996.

Walvoord, John F. *Holy Spirit: A Comprehensive Study of the Person and Work of the Holy Spirit.* Wheaton: Van Kampen Press, 1954.

Wenham, David. "Acts and the Pauline Corpus II: The Evidence of Parallels." *The Book of Acts in Its Ancient Literary Setting.* Ed. Bruce W. Winter and Andrew D. Clarke. The Book of Acts in Its First Century Setting 1. Grand Rapids: Eerdmans, 1993.

White, R. Fowler. "Gaffin and Grudem on Eph 2:20: In Defense of Gaffin's Exegesis." *Westminster Theological Journal* 54 (1992) 303-20.

Williams, D. J. *Acts.* New International Biblical Commentary 5. Peabody, MA: Hendrickson, 1990.

Witherington III, Ben. *The Acts of the Apostles: A Socio-Rhetorical Commentary.* Grand Rapids: Eerdmans/Carlisle, UK: Paternoster, 1998.

Wright, David F. "Why Were the Montanists Condemned?" *Themelios* 2 (1976) 15-22.

# OTHER BOOKS BY CHRISTIAN PUBLISHING HOUSE

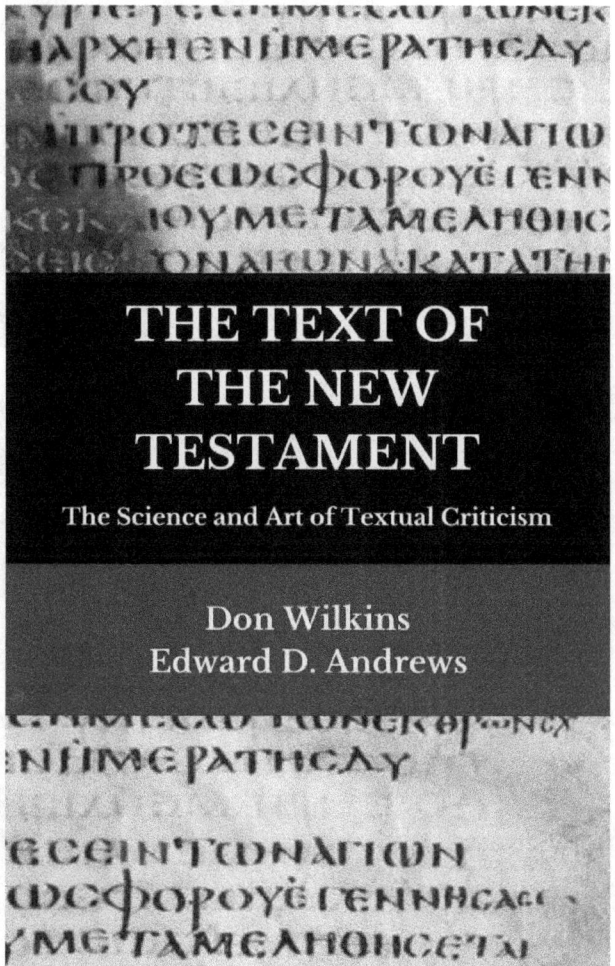

ISBN-10: 1-945757-44-2
ISBN-13: 978-1-945757-44-0

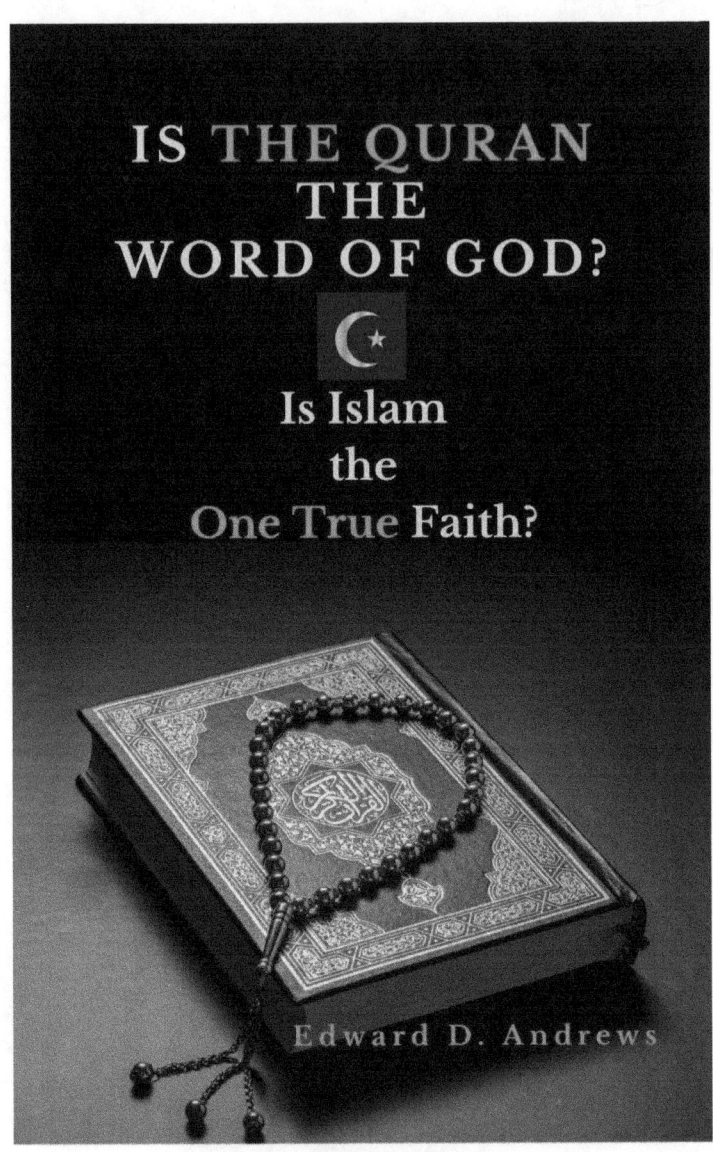

ISBN-13: 978-1-945757-49-5
ISBN-10: 1-945757-49-3

ISBN-13: 978-1-945757-61-7
ISBN-10: 1-945757-61-2

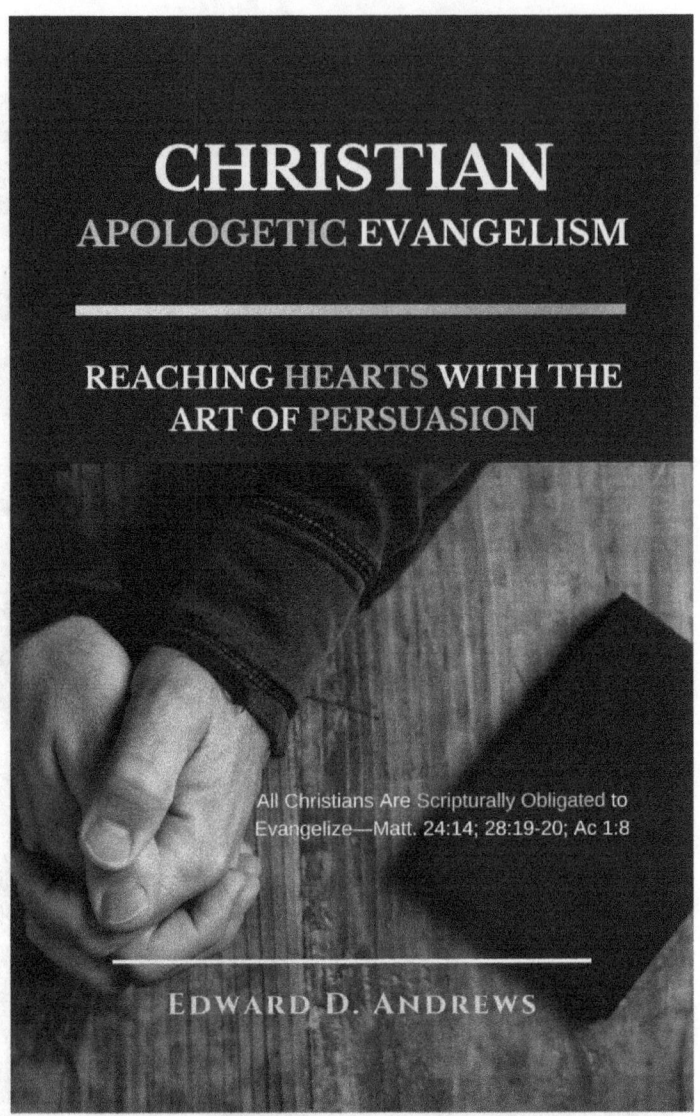

ISBN-13: 978-1-945757-75-4
ISBN-10: 1-945757-75-2

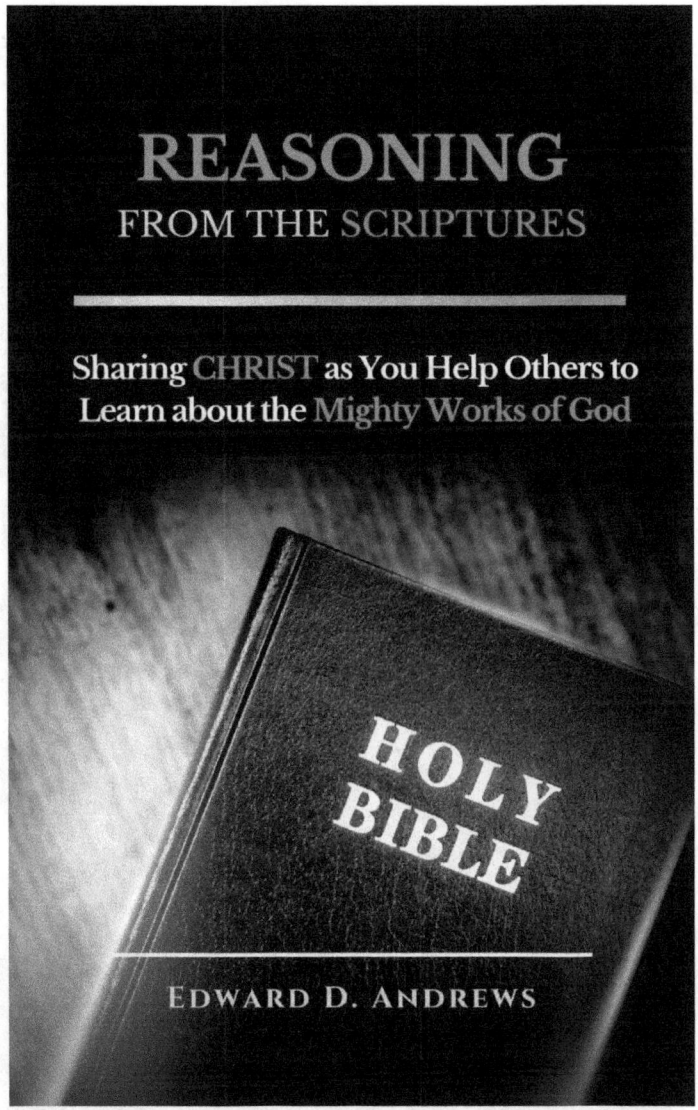

ISBN-13: 978-1-945757-82-2

ISBN-10: 1-945757-75-2

ISBN-13: 978-1-945757-81-5
ISBN-10: 1-945757-81-7

ISBN-13: 978-1-945757-40-2

ISBN-10: 1-945757-40-X

# THE CHURCH COMMUNITY IN CONTEMPORARY CULTURE

Evangelism and Engagement with Postmodern People

KIERAN BEVILLE

ISBN-10: 0692637680
ISBN-13: 978-0692637685

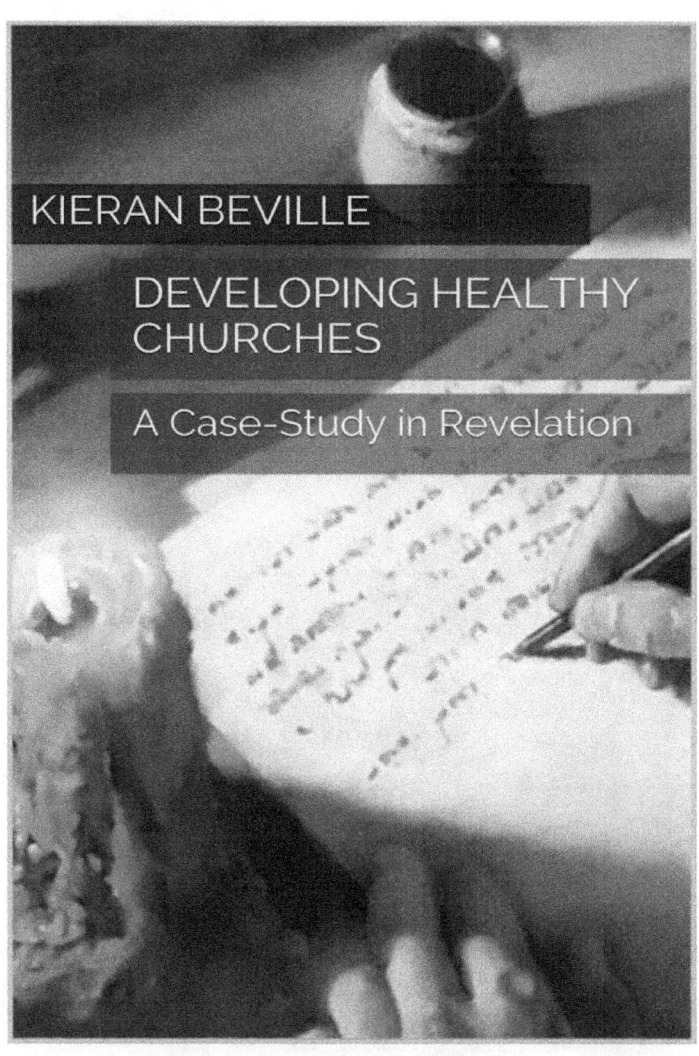

ISBN-10: 0692342982
ISBN-13: 978-0692342985

ISBN-13: 978-1-945757-43-3
ISBN-10: 1-945757-43-4

www.ingramcontent.com/pod-product-compliance
Lightning Source LLC
Chambersburg PA
CBHW070606050426
42450CB00011B/3007